DOG SECRETS

As Whispered to the Dog Sitter

Blenda R. Pilon, BSc, MSc

Dog Sitter, Author, Minister

Copyright © 2013 Blenda R. Pilon

Smashwords Edition, License Notes

ISBN- 0976277344
ISBN 9780976277347

Original photos by Blenda R. Pilon and dog owners.
Photos converted to grayscale by Danny Weeds.
Front cover design by Penelope Arden and Raymond Pilon.
Full cover layout by Esther Hart.

Published by Anchor Counseling

Other books by Blenda R. Pilon:
Falling in Love and Staying in Love
Change Your Thoughts, Change Your Waistline
(co-authored by Raymond Pilon)

www.DogSecretsWhispered.com

Dedication and Acknowledgements

I dedicate this book to all dog lovers!

I give special thanks for their love & support to:

Raymond, my husband and best friend

Max, now residing in Rainbow Bridge

The exquisite dogs I have dog-sat

Dog owners who have entrusted

their dogs to me.

Also Special Thanks to:

Cat Uhlin, Jan Thirlwall and Raymond for their expert editing

Loesje Jacob, Julia Bindas and Joyce & Eric Powell who endorsed my book

My family: Skip & Denise Rowland, Karen Wilcox and Frank Donnelly

My God Mother: Sandy Levey-Lunden; My God-children: Glenn Hamilton, Jan Thirwall, TjanaWitt and Elie Miskey

Also: Bette Parent, Andy Parent & Rena Eastwood, Sandra Pilon, Cecile & Lee Edes, and all Raymond's relatives.

Zoe Duff of Filidh Publishing for her consultation, editing and layout.

Esther Hart for knowledge and expertise when I really needed it to make my printing deadline.

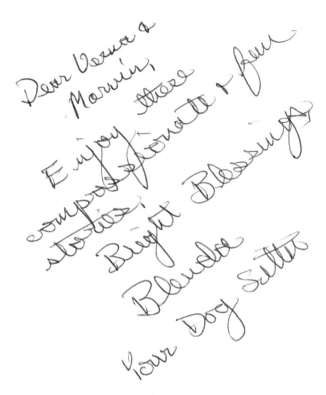

Table of Contents

DOG SECRETS as Whispered to the Dog Sitter

Forward

No subject has been more explored in all forms of media than the deep thriving desire for all human beings to develop and sustain relationships, be it between parent and child, brother and sister, friends, two people who want to share their lives together, or between humans and their pets. In this book, Blenda explores the fascinating relationship between humans and their dogs.

Never before have I met a human being, or should I say Spiritual Being, who exudes as much compassion as Blenda. The demonstration of this is easily observed in the caring way she treats dogs.

Blenda does not talk much about this, but I have witnessed miracles in some of her sessions with the dogs that she has dog sat over the years. In my opinion, anyone who has the foresight to have Blenda take care of their dogs, their "Precious Little Ones," are very lucky indeed. To Blenda, every dog is unique and special. She treats each and every dog with individual care, compassion, and the unconditional love that they richly deserve.

As Blenda's husband, I am deeply honored to have played a very small role in this amazing process of taking other peoples' little and big dogs into our home where we treat them like our own—with total love and compassion. But to be really clear, our exceptional dog sitting service is only made possible because of Blenda and her unwavering desire to treat these little critters with respect, honor, and unconditional love. Blenda believes that dogs are perfect, never at fault, and sometimes simply make little mistakes. It is easy to understand why dogs and dog sitting are Blenda's passion and forte. Blenda is a dynamic expression of love. I can vouch for this because as Blenda's husband I have experienced her awesome expression of love firsthand for twenty years…and it continues every day.

I know you'll find these stories inspiring, elevating and sometimes sad, but mostly just plain fun.

I am deeply honored to have played a very small part in this wonderful project.

I am confident that after reading Blenda's inspiring stories about the dogs she has been dog sitting over the past few years, you'll reach another level of love with your pets.

Perhaps you will even want to consult with Blenda about your dog, have her take care of your dogs, or even write a story about your dog or pet. Whatever you choose, I know your choice will provide you with an enriching experience beyond your wildest imagination.

I leave you with this thought, "It is done unto you as you believe." Sound familiar? I invite you to have fun, and "So It Is."

Rev. Raymond J Pilon

A Note from the Author

If the truth be known, I believe in our hearts we are children who like to play and cuddle. Perhaps this is why I love dogs and dog stories. Good stories about our four legged friends are much like the bed time stories I read as a little girl—those endearing stories that capture the heart. My stories remind me of this, and I am delighted to have the opportunity to share them with you.

As I started writing "***DOG SECRETS as Whispered to the Dog Sitter***," I discovered a central theme. Every dog my husband and I have encountered has taught us something. Since my driving passion is to learn more about Unconditional Love, I was most pleasantly surprised when I discovered my book's central theme is *How Dogs Teach us Unconditional Love*. Although we know many of the secrets, when they are delivered from dogs they take on special meaning. To make the secrets more acceptable, frequently the dogs reveal them in a hilarious way, such as when the young Boxer jumped over our four foot fence like it was nothing at all.

As you read these stories, I expect some will warm your heart, some will make you laugh, and some will make you cry. I am honored that the dogs have made me a vessel through which they whisper their secrets. They whisper through their unique dog language and behaviors. After dog sitting or being around dogs a lot, one naturally learns how to be a good DOG LISTENER. This is an art in itself. These stories will help educate you in this new and exciting adventure.

Just for the fun of it, if you have a story you would like to share about the secrets your dogs have shared (whispered) to you, please visit the section in my website http://www.dogsecretswhispered.com under *DOG SECRETS BOOK, Submit Your Story*. Please read through the submission requirements. You can contact me personally by emailing DogSecrets1@gmail.com. The secrets can be secrets your dog(s) have revealed through their adventures, humor, joy, mischief, love, loyalty, courage, experiences with children and heroism. In my upcoming books, I plan to include stories from other dog lovers. All ages from the youngest to the oldest may participate. I invite you to submit your stories.

Love and bright blessings,

Blenda R. Pilon, BSc, MSc, Centers for Spiritual Living, retired minister

PS: Some names in the dog stories have been changed to insure privacy.

Who Is in Charge?

(I include this story of Max because Max was our dog for seventeen years. His spirit continues to live on in my husband's and my hearts. A picture of him hangs proudly in our front hallway. Max and I communicate frequently. His loving Spirit guides me and all dogs and their owners who visit in our home.)

Is it possible our pets tell us
when it is time to go?

After you have read this story, you decide.

Max was our 17 year old Border-Collie/Black Lab. When Max was alive, Raymond, my husband, fondly told everyone he met, "Max is the most peaceful Being we have ever encountered, never showing one moment of aggression."

Here is my story about Max during his last months with us:

My gardening was finished and it was time for Max and me to go inside. Max tried getting up and collapsed. His legs wouldn't support him. After resting 10 minutes, I tried coaxing Max to climb the stairs. Max tried but still couldn't get up.

A strong neighbor came to the rescue. She picked up our

seventy pound Max and climbed the steep back stairs while assuring him, "It's OK, big boy." Gently my neighbor laid Max down on his blanket in the living room.

When it was bedtime, we dreaded having to leave Max in the living room by himself. As if reading our thoughts, Max rose up on all fours and literally dragged himself into the bedroom. During the night, Max frequently got up to change positions. Intuitively, I knew his pain was intense. My heart went out to Max, and as it did, my heart felt like it was enlarging in its capacity to love. I watched as a stream of white effervescent light issued forth from my heart and engulfed Max.

When I awakened the next morning, I lingered in bed because I dreaded what seemed like *the inevitable day*. I prayed for a miracle. After much discussion, Raymond agreed to give Max one more chance. Max heard us and seized the opportunity. He hobbled down the stairs and walked slowly across the street to do his business in the bushes.

Victorious, Raymond and I quickly agreed Max deserved to stay on this planet. Again Max heard us and thanked us with kisses. After this experience, we decided to get our big "know-it-all" selves out of the way and let Max's Spirit tell us when he was ready to make his transition.

As if to test us, later in the morning Raymond was in the back yard. Max was restless so I purposely left the back porch door open. Max walked onto the porch, surveyed the approximate thirteen steps to the ground and started climbing down the steep stairs. Raymond shouted, "What in the world are you doing?"

From the tone of his voice I believed Raymond thought I was nuts. I didn't think so. After all, we had surrendered the inevitable decision—leaving its timing to Max. In a light-hearted defensive tone I replied, "Everything is fine. Max wanted to come see you."

I quickly disappeared inside before Raymond could say another word.

Fifteen minutes later Max decided to come inside. He climbed all thirteen backstairs on his own. We were amazed.

**"Never give up. Just give me a chance
and as long as you love and trust me,
I'll do my best."**

Yes, Max's actions spoke loudly: "Never give up. Just give me a chance, and as long as you love and trust me, I'll do my best. I love you guys and I love dog life. Yes, I'm a miracle dog, but then there are a whole lot of miracle dogs and people that perform miracles when we give enough love, enough prayers, and enough trust. Now I'm going to go beg for some of those delicious chicken munchies. Ah! Life is good!"

Thank goodness Max spoke up before we mistakenly took him to the Vet. He let us know it wasn't his time.

**When the Spirit within us that is the real
driving force wants to live, the Spirit
performs miracles. This holds true for dogs,
for people, for all life!**

Two days later Max surprised us again. Sensing Max was in great pain, I decided to give him half an Ibuprofen tablet at night. I knew too much could make his tummy bleed, but I believed that since I had just started giving Max Ibuprofen it would be OK. Max wanted me to know different. He ate all of his dinner and carefully deposited the half tablet, not chewed, by the side of his empty dish. This time I got the message. Max knew what was best for him

Many days later Max showed signs of further slowing down. Raymond and I were determined to listen to the signs of what Max was saying, and if it got too rough,

4

we would take Max to the vet. We didn't know how long Max could continue living his doggy life. What we did recognize was that every moment spent with our dog was precious. Raymond and I honored Max's path, his decisions, and our invitation to listen.

TWO WEEKS LATER: Raymond and I enjoyed two glorious weeks together with Max, petting him and simply sharing our love. Then one day Max looked deeply into both our eyes, and at a soul level whispered his Truth—he was ready to make his transition. Raymond and I respected Max's decision. In his own doggie language Max asked that we share his last wish. Max's wish is that we (and that includes you) benefit from his experience by knowing:

"Miracles happen as we trust in the power of Love!"

Tink
What a Character!

My husband and I have dog sat many dogs. When we received Tink, we knew we had accepted a very unusual dog into our care. Tink was a seven year old female Pug. She came from a large East Indian family where there were plenty of people to keep her company.

It was late summer. Tink came into our home sniffing it out. She couldn't seem to get her bearings. Tink's parents had brought her blanket which we put in the living room. When she was lying on her blanket, Tink couldn't see what I was doing in the kitchen. Of course, this made Tink feel isolated. Ninety percent of what I do takes place in the kitchen. This is where my office/computer is set up, as well as where all cooking takes place. Men hide out in their caves, but I have an open-amphitheater "come-disturb-me" cozy combo of kitchen & office. Normally I don't mind if dogs disturb me while I am in my kitchen/office because it adds a touch of love. Unfortunately, Tink was sticking close to her blanket where she couldn't see me. I recalled that her owner, named Lorraine, had told me that Tink is not allowed in the kitchen. Not being able to see me combined with training not to be in the kitchen created quite a dilemma for Tink.

Tink stared fiercely into my eyes beseeching my Soul. Through her gaze she asked me, "How could you do this to me?"

In an effort to help Tink, I decided to tempt her to feel safe coming into my kitchen. To accomplish my mission, I put Tink's food in a dish near where I sat in the kitchen. She walked slowly to the dish, smelled the food, and then began snorting. Tink stared fiercely into my eyes, as if beseeching my Soul. Through her gaze she asked me, "How could you do this to me?"

I didn't understand what I was doing that disturbed Tink so much. After standing and snorting before her dish several times, Tink walked away. Her dish stood full— not a drop of food touched. I was mystified.

I pondered, "What is wrong? Have I done something mean? If so, I would like to know what it is."

Several hours later while I was cooking, I guessed what was bothering this unusual fur ball. Tink wasn't eating was because I was using our dog dish. I was not using her special dog dish that her Mom had given me. I reasoned, "Yes, this could be the answer!"

Immediately I switched dishes and put Tink's dog food in her own dish. Then I called her. This time Tink sauntered cautiously into the kitchen, went over to her dish and quickly started gulping down her food. WOW! The mystery was solved.

Tink wanted to eat out of her own dog dish rather than some other dog's dish.

Tink snuggled into her blankets. Within the minute, she the loudest snores that I have ever heard from a dog bellowed forth.

Next hurdle was Tink at bedtime. She wanted to sleep with us, Raymond and myself, in our bedroom at the foot of our bed. Tink snuggled into her blankets. Within the minute, she bellowed forth the loudest snores that I have ever heard from a dog. Raymond was beside himself as he said, "How am I ever going to sleep with that monstrous noise?"

A few minutes later Tink took a little break from her snoring. Luckily this provided just the opportunity Raymond needs to fall asleep. Unfortunately for me, though, I tossed and turned as I listened to the symphony of snoring: first Tink, then Raymond. After Tink finally reached the peak of her snore and it was starting to soften, that was when Raymond would start into his snore which got progressively louder until it reached its peak. Tink and Raymond were in total synch as they were trumpeting a symphonic duet. I was their captive audience.

For a long time I lay listening in quiet amazement. Finally I said to myself, "I've had enough of this. There is no logical reason for me to be a captive audience/prisoner." I went over to my ghetto blaster, turned on my meditation music, and concentrated on it until I blotted out their snoring. In peaceful gratitude, I fell asleep.

Well, you know, I really can't blame Tink. Because Pugs have short snouts, it is difficult for them to breathe. Snoring and snorting comes quite naturally to Pugs. As I also discovered, this can present problems when walking Pugs.

I shall now share with you Tink's and my walking experience. I cleverly designed a chain on which I can walk three dogs at once. Using my clever chain, I started out on a walk with Tink, the little Chihuahua, and the Pomeranian that were in my care. The walk I chose was into Goldstream Park. It is a long walk down to the stream followed by a steep hike back up the hill. Tink was doing some huffing going down the hill, but on her return up the steep hill she developed a shortness of breath. She started choking which necessitated our stopping every couple of minutes to relax so she could catch her breath. By the time I returned home I made up my mind that in all fairness to Tink, her walks should take place on level ground. From that time forward, she got to walk on level ground. Frequently Tink got her own special walk. The other dogs preferred to let off their steam taking more adventuresome walks with lots of hills.

> *I knew I would miss her following me around the house, snuggling up next to me when I watched television, her snorting, and even her snoring.*

On the whole, Tink had a great time and seemed to really enjoy socializing with the other dogs. Her Mom, Lorraine, said Tink wasn't very friendly with other dogs. This seven day visit seemed to prove her wrong. When Tink's owners came to pick her up, she was happy to see them; and yet to show her appreciation, Tink came over to me and Raymond for a farewell lick as if to say, "Good bye, and thank you for the great time." With her fond good bye, I forgave Tink for all her strange behaviors. I knew I would miss her following me around the house, snuggling up next to me when I watched television, her snorting, and even her snoring.

Well, wouldn't you know it, shortly before Christmas I got a phone call wondering if Raymond and I would take Tink for Christmas. The other dog who was supposed to come had just backed out, so my intuition told me that we were supposed to have Tink as our Christmas dog. Raymond and I accepted.

Tink came bounding up to our front door on December 24th. When we opened the door, Tink practically leaped into our arms greeting us with a big lick. Honestly, I was astounded. I didn't think Tink would remember us, no less care so much. Being a sucker for receiving love, her display of love set me off on the right foot.

> ***Tink acted like she did not know what to do with a squeak toy, and could not comprehend she was getting a gift for her very own.***

We were very busy setting up the Christmas tree and wrapping presents. Tink was having fun being our shadow and following us around. As if Tink knew we needed our sleep on Christmas Eve, she curled up into the bed we made for her. She snored so softly that our music quickly put us to sleep. On Christmas Day, Tink's Chihuahua friend came over with her Mom. We all enjoyed opening presents together. I tend to believe this was the first Christmas that Tink had been given gifts from under the tree. We gave her a squeak toy as a gift. It took her many attempts before she learned how to wrap her mouth around the rubber squeaker to squeak it. Tink acted as if she could not comprehend she was getting a gift for her very own. The second gift we gave Tink was turkey wrapped in gift paper. After briefly sniffing the gift-wrapped turkey, she wasted no time digging right into it.

Tink's human big brother came to pick her up on December 28th. I mistakenly believed Tink's human family would be picking her up on the 29th. I was sad when they arrived early. Suddenly the house seemed very empty without Tink, my faithful shadow.

I started recalling some fond memories of my time with Tink. I recalled one morning when Tink standing over her dishes and talking to me. It took me a long while, but finally I heard what she was saying. She wanted some fresh water. I went over to her water dish and took it to the tap getting her some fresh water. When I put down the dish, Tink gulped down the water like there was no tomorrow. No doubt about it—fresh water was what Tink wanted. She had sense enough to know that if she kept talking to me, sooner or later I would get her message. I'm sure she was thinking, "After all, why should a princess have to drink stale water that is a day old? I deserve the best!"

The day after Tink left, on December29th, I received a phone call from Lorraine. She told me that her husband said Tink was getting to be too much for them to handle. She explained that there were three people in their family who were allergic to dogs. Lorraine believed they would have to find another home for Tink. She wondered if I could help.

My heart sank. I could not take Tink, but promised I would write my dog friends asking if anyone of them might take Tink. At this moment, I realized that even with all her peculiar perks, Tink gave me the most special gift of all. She gave my husband and me unconditional love. In return, all Tink wanted from us was food, fresh water and to be treated with loving respect.

I thought, "I know that there is a group of people who really love pugs. I will pray that one of them will discover Tink and provide her with a loving home to live out the rest of her adult life."

> *Tink helped me to really "get it," that each dog was whispering a special secret to me. Tink taught me that if a dog seems strange at first, keep looking.*

As I contacted my friends, I realized how blessed Raymond and I were to have shared a warm, loving Christmas with Tink. Because of her predicament and with gratitude to Tink, I decided to write up some of my dog sitting memories. Tink helped me to really "get it," that each dog was whispering a special secret to me. Tink taught me that if a dog seems strange at first, keep looking. Each dog has a very special gift that it is offering. With Tink it was her unconditional love, her following me around the house keeping me company, and her daring to confide her delightful requests and secrets.

And What Happened to Tink?

After asking around, I found one caring woman who thought Tink would be wonderful for her parents. Then she learned her parents were moving and would not be able to take Tink. Another lady, who lives near me, said that if no home was found for Tink, she would talk to her husband and see if they could take in Tink. This would bring their total number of dogs to five. She said she only wanted to do take Tink if it were a last resort.

I talked further with Lorraine. From the compassion in her voice, it was easy to tell that she really wanted to keep Tink. She said they were trying to work out a plan, and she would get back to me. She emphasized that the main reason for the family's concern was that many people in her home were allergic to dogs. I invited Lorraine to call me if she had further need.

Many months passed. Lorraine called me. I was thrilled that she and her family had decided to keep Tink. After chatting, Raymond and I were given another opportunity to dog sit Tink. We couldn't wait to see her again. I met Lorraine and her husband half way to our home so they would not have to drive so far. When I saw Tink she remembered me and squealed a good portion of the way home. Once home, Tink officially greeted me by jumping into my arms. Once again, this melted my heart. This time, we had three other dogs staying with us. Tink befriended all three. Because she makes many strange noises, the other dogs had to sniff and investigate her. She passed their exam with flying colors. When we took our walks together on level ground, Tink lagged somewhat behind. She did a lot of grunting and groaning as she was having difficulty peeing and pooing. The other dogs seemed to understand, were willing to wait for her, and even perked up their ears when she made her special squeals that were distinctive by their high pitched ring.

I have to hand it to Tink. Obviously, she had arrived with a urinary infection that was in its infancy, and therefore was not detected by her owners. Once at our home, Tink became increasing uncomfortable, often rubbing her fanny against the carpet and floor.

Frequently she begged to go outside, including three times during the middle of the night. Although sometimes Tink was successful in peeing, the majority of times her peeing attempts failed. When it didn't work, pressure would build up. Feeling miserable and exhausted, Tink was not able to control herself. Pressure would build up until she suddenly burst forth with a huge puddle of pee. Both Raymond and I cleaned up being sure we never criticized her. After all, Tink was doing her best.

Tink's owners were out of reach via their cell phones. I called their Veterinarian who said that the urinary infection could probably wait. On the other hand, the Veterinarian's office sternly advised that if Tink could not poop, we should bring her to their clinic immediately.

This recommendation prompted me to put on my thinking cap. I called a local pet store, and they suggested giving Tink pumpkin seed to regulate her bowel movements. I then called the relative who was the emergency contact for Tink. After discussing the predicament and the different options that had been presented to me, we mutually agreed that the best temporary solution was to implement the pumpkin seed remedy.

Tink seemed to understand and accept our decision. She never complained, and under the circumstances of not feeling well, did an exceptional job of always being cheerful with the other dogs. Of course, Raymond and I reassured Tink that she was loved.

When you are deeply committed to one another your relationship grows, you each grow, and everyone around you prospers. This is true for humans with humans, as well as for humans with their fur ball friends.

When Tink's family came to pick up Tink, I believe they planned to take her that day to the Vet. Tink was happy to see her family. The young boy who was her human brother made a bed for Tink beside him in the passenger seat of the car. Tink seemed content to curl up next to him.

Myself, I was again counting my blessings that Raymond and I were endowed with loving hands and hearts, thus enabling us to nurse Tink at her time of need. When you love someone (whether human, dog, or whatever kind of pet), I find it is always a two-way street. You are there for each other when times are great as well as when they are tough. As a relationship therapist for seventeen years, I learned that the number one reason that marriages fail is that one or both of the parties believe that if things don't work out there is a back door for escape. Conversely, partners who enjoy successful relationships believe that when the going gets tough you communicate until you work your way through the hurdles. When you are deeply committed to one another, your relationship grows, you each grow, and everyone around you prospers. This is true for humans with humans, as well as for humans with their fur ball friends.

Doggie in the Window

When I was a little girl, and that was a long time ago, I used to love the song "How Much Is That Doggie in the Window…Arf, Arf, the One with the Waggly Tail?" I would picture the perfect puppy dog looking out of the store window, so adorable that when passing by the store window, no one would be able to resist admiring the dog. When Eric and Joyce brought us Riley, I knew Riley was the irresistible puppy dog that, as a child, I had pictured in the imaginary store window.

The way I see it, Riley's purpose was to help heal his new Mother.

Indeed, Riley is a perfect picture puppy. Riley is a pure white Bichon Poo, and was three years old when his human dog parents entrusted him to us (Raymond and me) for dog sitting. I say "entrusted" because we were the first dog sitters that Joyce and Eric dared trust enough to try out as dog sitters. Riley's parents told us that Riley would probably experience some separation anxiety when they left him with us. Eric explained why. He said that because Joyce had been very sick and wanted a dog for healing, he had agreed to let a dog enter into their lives. Literally, Riley was selected for a definite purpose. The way I see it, Riley's purpose was to help heal his new Mother.

Day after day Joyce lay in her bed incapacitated/unable to get up, and day by day Riley was by his Mom's side. Riley would snuggle with his Mom showering her with magical doggie unconditional love.

The moment Riley arrived was the moment Joyce's miraculous healing began. With Riley patiently attending to his patient's needs, every day Joyce improved until finally she could get up, walk around, and even leave home to visit her children and Grandchildren.

I know that many men would break under the intense affection that Riley was giving his new Mom.

Having been a relationship therapist by profession, I know that many men would break under the intense affection that Riley was giving his new Mom. Their self-esteem would take a kicking, and they would become jealous of the dog. This was not the case with Eric. Eric was grateful for Riley and made sure that he gave Riley emotional support so *Therapeutic Nurse* Riley would not burn out. Eric praised this new sensitive, caring *Canine Spirit*. He attended to Riley's needs making sure he ate nutritious food, had many walks, and was nurtured with special male "man-to-man" bonding.

As I recall Riley's first day with my husband and me, I truly have to laugh. Never have I met such a sensitive dog. Never have I met a dog suffering from such a high level of anxiety separation. Never have I met such an adorable "doggie-in-the-window". All three of these delightful *nevers* were packed into one dog, and this dog was actually at our home. Our first day of dog sitting was scheduled for five hours.

As soon as Riley's parents left on this first day of dog sitting, Riley rushed to the big stuffed chair sitting by the window. Riley sat up on the chair and positioned himself so he could look out our living room window. When his parents' car pulled out of the driveway and Riley saw the car fade into the distance, Riley started whining.

After listening to the whining for half an hour, Raymond said, "Won't this dog ever stop? I can't take this anymore—the poor thing!"

Trying to relieve Riley of his anxiety, I went over to Riley and began petting him. Riley responded by jumping down off the chair and running to the hall-way entrance by the front door. Sitting all alone in the front entrance and looking like he lost his best friend, Riley continued his mournful whining.

We liked to think he was being friendly, but the truthful reality was that Riley was simply jumping up on the chair so he was tall enough to see out the window.

Raymond and I discussed what to do, and decided that if we ignored Riley he might get tired of whining. Rather than reward or punish Riley, we agreed that we ignore him. We figured using this approach that Riley would not feel pressured and eventually would be brave enough to venture upstairs. After an hour passed of listening to Riley's mournful whining, he climbed slowly up the stairs and began exploring his new surroundings. The first thing Riley did in his explorations was to pee on the coverlet I had on the living room couch. Understanding that Riley was nervous, I decided to overlook his misbegotten behavior. I did, however, pick up Riley, put him gently in my arms and carry him outside to the back porch. Much to my surprise, Riley climbed down our thirteen back porch stairs. Sniffing the air that was filled with the fresh scent of pine needles, Riley began a thorough investigation of our large back yard.

When Riley finally returned to the house, he seemed more content. He meandered into the bedroom, jumped up on the bed, and literally hid out in self-imposed solitary confinement. Every once in a while, however, Riley would bless us with his presence and return to the living room long enough to jump up on the living room chair. We liked to think he was being friendly, but the truthful reality was that Riley was simply jumping up on the chair so he was tall enough to see out the window. Of course, he was checking to see if his parents were in sight.

Talk about being psychic, Riley takes the cake. About half an hour before his parents arrived, Riley again began whining. Nothing could distract him. A couple minutes before Joyce and Eric arrived at the house, Riley put his paws up on the window sill so he could rest his nose against the window pane for a bird's-eye-view. This time Riley knew beyond any shadow of doubt that his parents would soon arrive to take him home. When their car pulled into the driveway, you have never seen a dog howl and dance like Riley. When we opened the front door, Riley literally jumped into Joyce's and Eric's arms.

After this awesome first experience with Riley, Raymond wasn't sure we should take Riley again. He said, "Riley is too queasy and too sensitive." Then Raymond added, "Besides, Riley obviously doesn't like me; he runs away every time I come anywhere near him."

While I understood Raymond's concerns, I felt compelled to express my own feelings. I replied, "Just give Riley a chance. He is super-sensitive and a wonderful dog. His parents have entrusted Riley to us. I don't want to break that trust. Besides, I really like Riley."

Raymond agreed that we would take Riley at least one

more time. I realized that the reason I liked Riley so much was because he is super-sensitive. I remembered a psychological test I took in college where I was tested as being in the 99% bracket of being the most sensitive of those people in the test group. I was informed that my best and worst trait was my sensitivity. Ever since receiving this test result and becoming acutely aware of my high level of sensitivity, I bond easily with sensitive dogs and people.

Riley and I were both super-sensitive and I found myself loving Riley for mirroring via his Dog Hood my own sensitivity.

Riley and I were both super-sensitive, and I found myself loving Riley for mirroring via his Dog Hood my own sensitivity. I couldn't wait to dog sit Riley again. I knew Raymond and I would ultimately be able to provide an atmosphere of trust for Riley—trust away from home. I didn't know how Riley would change after he learned to trust us, but I liked to imagine that it would be good.

Riley's parents had work that often called them out of the house and required dog sitting for four or five hours at a time. After many visits with us, Riley started relaxing. He even began coming over to both Raymond and me to get a pet.

You may recall that, during the first day of dog sitting, Riley would run away every time Raymond got near him. Now after extending our patience and tender loving care to Riley, his new demonstration of trust in

Raymond brought a well-earned, triumphant smile to Raymond's face.

Although for the first couple of times dog sitting Riley there were no other dogs that we were caring for, soon the inevitable happened. The first dog Riley encountered was another white Bichon dog named Buddy, who was also three years old. The match couldn't have been more perfect. Being more assertive and friendly, Buddy walked over to Riley and gently nuzzled Riley with his wet nose. Much to our delight, Riley responded by standing still and accepting the welcoming nuzzle. Before long, both dogs were chasing round the house.

Riley seemed happy to discover a playmate with whom he could play. If I could read Riley's mind based on his behavior, he would be saying, "For so long I have had healing responsibilities that I forgot what it was like to be a puppy dog. This is great stuff. I really dig being a puppy dog. Thanks for being my friend, Buddy. Let's go play!"

Riley had dedicated so much of his life to being a Therapeutic Nurse; well, it choked me up with tears of joy to see Riley playing like a little dog with his new dog friend.

Silly, they were only dogs, but as I watched Riley and Buddy chase around the home, my heart got very warm. Since Riley had dedicated so much of his life to being a *Therapeutic Nurse*; it choked me up with tears of joy to see Riley playing like a little dog with his new dog friend. To me, the feeling I was having was similar to

25

the feeling I have when a participant on American Idol, who has experienced a hard time in life, discovers they have a good singing voice and is chosen to go to Hollywood—I can't help but experiencing their joy and happiness.

> *I realized that it is not so much what we do for the dogs as it is the safe and caring atmosphere we create that makes a difference.*

Recognizing that Raymond and I helped create special moments like these through our dog sitting, it made our dog sitting more precious. Providing a safe and caring atmosphere for the dogs made me increasingly grateful for Raymond's and my loving relationship. I realized that it is not so much what we do for the dogs, as it is the safe and caring atmosphere we create that makes a difference. I believe Cesar Millan would agree. Cesar Millan teaches that calm, assertive energy is best for training dogs—it provides them with an environment conducive to carrying out their Canine Purpose.

Speaking of Canine Purpose, I think Riley and his family know that Riley has a definite purpose. Riley's purpose is to make sure his Mom is healthy and his Dad is happy. This is, indeed, a big job. Because of the nature of this big job, Riley tends to be somewhat humanized and highly dependent upon human contact for his Well Being. Treating dogs with unconditional love in the same way that dogs treat us with their unconditional love, I have come to the conclusion that it is okay for a dog to be humanized and long for human contact. What

26

really counts is the bottom line. The bottom line in dog-master relationships is that both dog and master(s) are happy. Heck! Who cares what that looks like "behavior-wise." What matters is the happiness.

I believe that the Ideal Family Relationship between Dog and Master should be a reflection of their "Mutually Shared Happiness".

This reminds me of an analogy. In the country called Bhutan that is nestled in the Himalayas, they have an economic policy called "Gross National Happiness" in which Happiness and Well-Being are the sought after Gross National Products. Using the Bhutanese policy as a prototype, I believe that the Ideal Family Relationship between Dog and Master should be a reflection of their *"Mutually Shared Happiness"*.

Because Riley has now been with us about once a week for a little over a year, we know Riley pretty well. In sharing with Riley, I have to admit that on my part it is heartwarming to have a dog who, when I am sitting on the couch, climbs up and puts his paws around my shoulders. Riley is such an affectionate dog and definitely has his preferences. With some dogs, he loves to play, while with other dogs he chooses to ignore them. Right now Riley is with two fourteen month old Great Danes, and while he is fine with them playing together, Riley doesn't enter into their play. Maybe it is because they are too young, or too big, or too this or that. Really it doesn't matter because Riley is happy and the Great Danes are happy. They are happy *just the way they are!*

As Louise Hays, author of **You can Heal Your Life** says, *"There is nothing to rearrange or change. You are perfect just the way you are!"*

When I think that I have progressed as far as I can developing my relationship with a fantastic dog such as Riley, I most often discover there is something new to learn or to add. After reading Cesar Millan's book **Short Guide to a Happy Dog,** I realized that Riley fits Cesar Millan's description of a Pack Leader both in the home and in his walking behaviors. As I reflected upon my own walking habits with Riley, I realized that when I have been walking Riley, he always walks ahead of me pulling me wherever he wants to go. Obviously, Riley has been the Pack Leader in control. Believing that having so much responsibility as a pack leader is not a good idea for a dog (it makes the dog carry the burden of responsibility), I am currently working on changing this situation by walking Riley on a short leash. As I walk I keep Riley either close beside me, or in back of me. Today as I was using this technique, I rewarded Riley with pets when he stopped yanking. The result was a third or more of the time we walked in synchronicity.

In unspoken words we have both intuitively agreed that our personal relationship is to be fun or not at all.

I think it is fun and mentally stimulating to have something new to learn and to do. Riley is great for being my partner in trying new things because he is super sensitive like I am. Being sensitive, we can read each other's thoughts, desires and behaviors quickly.

Intuitively I know when Riley has had enough of learning for the day, and instinctively Riley knows when I want to show him a new way of doing things. I honestly believe Riley trusts me enough to recognize that if he doesn't like what I am teaching, then he can say no in his own way and I will understand. If it is not good for Riley, then I will back off. In unspoken words we have both intuitively agreed that our personal relationship is to be fun or not at all. Oh yes, and I must add, Riley and I have further decided that whatever we learn and do needs to benefit the whole. The whole includes my relationship with my husband and Riley's number one relationship with his Human Mom and Dad. This is our solemn pledge made by me as an important Dog Sitter, and Riley as an important Canine Being!

By the way, I couldn't possibly end my story about Riley without confiding in you that Riley proves to be that adorable puppy dog I saw in the store window as a child. Funny, Riley looks so adorable that he looks like a stuffed dog that couldn't possibly be real.

Well, not only does Riley look adorable, but his cute antics have hit the top of the dog charts. Today when Raymond gave me a hug, Riley jumped up between us with both paws going up and down, and round and round in little circles, moving in perfect unison. This was Riley's way of demanding that he be included in our affection, in our hug.

Such is the Life of Riley. What a dog!

Who's at the End of the Leash?

A long time ago I saw a sign posted on the closed gate of the marina. When the gate was opened, it led down a steep gang plank to where many boats were anchored. The sign read, "DOGS BEWARE! CAUTION! All owners must be on a leash!"

As my husband and I dog sat Zora, I recalled this sign and wondered, "Was Zora on the end of the leash, or were Raymond and I on the end of the leash? Were we training Zora, or was she training us?"

I wondered, "Will I be able to handle this big adorable brute of overzealous puppy dog?

Cole Fleming was going away, across the Pacific Ocean, to Singapore to outfit a boat and make good money. Since Cole wasn't driving, he asked us to visit his home that was thirty miles away. He wanted us to meet him and his dog, Zora, prior to dog sitting. Thanks to GPS we found Cole's home, but there was a maximum five minutes parking outside. If we stayed longer, we would be liable for towing and a steep fine. Aware of these parking restrictions, Raymond and I decided we would make it a quick interview. Cole and Zora were waiting for us. Zora, with all the playfulness of a ten month old Boxer, danced around at the sight of us. She even tried jumping up on me. Being a mere five feet tall, I coaxed Zora to jump on Raymond instead of me. Zora promptly complied almost knocking him over. Raymond recovered and started playing with Zora.

Cole explained that Zora was overzealous when she first meets new people, and that being just a puppy she would soon calm down. I believed Cole, but I have to admit I was a bit suspicious of this playful Boxer. When I gave her a medium sized bowl of her dog food, she finished it in two big gulps. Although Cole had asked me to feed Zora as a way of impressing me, instead it made me suspicious of what would be required to take care of this high-strung, ravishingly hungry fur ball. I wondered, "Will I be able to handle this big adorable brute of overzealous puppy dog?

Wanting to please this young loving dog owner, Cole, who seemed set on us taking Zora, I put aside my suspicions. Raymond and I agreed that we would dog sit Zora for three weeks while Cole was overseas.

Cole arrived at our house late one March evening with Zora. As if announcing her arrival, Zora raced around our little home. Within the first five minutes, she had knocked down a massage table leaning against the wall with a huge "THUD!" Once again, I shoved aside my intuition that was warning me that dog sitting Zora would be a huge mistake. I reassured Cole everything would be fine until he returned. With a friend waiting in the truck, Cole departed quickly.

"Okay! I'm here and all yours. Now let's play! Party time!!!"

Once Zora heard Cole's car pull out of the driveway, she began exploring the house. She promptly ate a large raw hide bone that we had accidently left unguarded on the floor, and then returned jumping up on us as if to say, "Okay! I'm here and all yours. Now let's play! Party time!"

But, heck, what could I do when Zora looked at me with her adorable big brown eyes peering out of her strange looking Boxer face? In a weird way Zora looked so unbecoming she was beautiful.

Boxers are big dogs. Because I am little, I don't want big dogs such as Zora jumping up on me and possibly knocking me over. It was all I could do to push Zora from me. I was determined to stand my ground, and finally Zora got my message. Surrendering, she decided to curl up next to me on the couch with her head on my lap like a little puppy dog—which certainly she was not. But, heck, what could I do when Zora looked at me with her adorable big brown eyes peering out of her strange looking Boxer face? In a weird way, Zora looked so unbecoming she was beautiful.

Since dog sitting is my business and my husband just supports my whims, I am usually the person who does the dog walking. With Zora, however, I asked Raymond to help with the walking. I figured that after Raymond first took Zora for a walk, I could learn from him how to walk a BIG, undisciplined dog.

We soon discovered that Cole left no harness, only a leash. The next day when Raymond opened the front door, Zora raced outside like she had never been out on a W-A-L-K before. This began the battle of wits. I never saw Raymond have to yank so hard and often. Frequently Zora refused to obey Raymond's commands. Following a long and strenuous walk, Raymond complained, "Walking Zora is worse than training a horse." And then after a moment of reflection, Raymond added, "But then again, maybe she is teaching me patience!"

Examining Raymond's red arms that were very sore from the yanking, I was convinced there was absolutely no way that I could walk this brute of a dog.

Feeling remiss in my pledge to Raymond that I would walk the dogs, I went to the pet store and bought a harness to which the saleslady instructed me to attach the leash on the bottom hook under the collar. She explained that the hook was strategically positioned at the bottom of the collar in order to provide more control to the person walking the dog. I told Raymond what the saleslady said, but he didn't see the sense in it.

Raymond hooked Zora's leash to the top (not the bottom like the saleslady suggested) of the harness. Although this gave Raymond some control while walking Zora, there still ensued a tug-of-war between man and beast.

"My Goodness!" Zora was telling Raymond, "After all, I'm a mere pup who wants to run and play. Won't you understand? What must I do to train you?"

Despite his puppy antics, day by day life with Zora began calming down, that is, until Friday. Rather sheepishly I reminded Raymond we had consented to dog sit another dog for the week end....a six year old Lab and Rockweiler mix named Roxy.

Early Saturday morning, Karen, Roxy's owner , knocked at the front door with her dog. I asked her to please go toward the back gate and wait until Raymond got to the back yard where we would let both dogs run off some steam and get acquainted. When Roxy entered the back yard, Zora started running around faster than I have ever seen a dog run. Scared stiff, I let myself out of the back yard gate leaving Karen and Raymond, who were far braver than I was, to fend off the dogs. It seems I got to safety just in the nick of time. Zora raced toward Roxy.

Taking a big lunge forward, she began attacking Roxy who was by far the bigger dog.

Alarmed Karen exclaimed, "This is the first time I have seen Roxy intimidated and start defending herself."

Raymond said, "Don't worry; the two dogs are just doing their one upmanship thing to see who is going to be the winner—the boss."

I was standing outside the fence panicked. Raymond, who was inside the fence, watched with a smile on his face that said he believed the two dogs were simply working out their dominance issues. Raymond advised me, "Don't worry; the two dogs are just doing their one upmanship thing to see who is going to be the winner—the boss."

Well, guess what? Raymond was right. Soon Roxy had the uncontrollable Zora pinned down on her back with belly upright in the total submissive position. *THAT WAS IT...FIGHT OVER!* Roxy was the boss. The dominance decision had been settled. Within moments the two dogs were playing like best friends.

I was totally amazed how quickly the two dogs worked out their dominance issues...certainly not like humans who often take years to figure out who is boss. As Raymond later pointed out, "At no time was there any physical jaw or body contact."

Anyway, with this dominance issue decided, Karen left for the week end. With Karen gone, the two dogs begged to come inside. What a rumpus! It felt like we were in the middle of a stampede with two wild stallions loose in our living room. Raymond and I flew around making sure all the glasses and coffee mugs were safely taken off the tables where most likely they would be knocked down. After what seemed like an hour, but in reality was probably only ten to fifteen minutes, Roxy, who was now the pack leader, got tired.

"Thank goodness," I thought as I heaved a big sigh of relief.

Roxy must have picked up my thoughts because she growled at Zora, and Zora finally settled down. "Thank Goodness!" I thought to myself, "At last I can get some well-deserved peace."

The next day Raymond decided to walk Roxy and leave Zora in the back yard. He was gone five minutes when there was a knock at the front door. A man was standing before me with his Golden Retriever. I shuddered, "Oh my God! I didn't accept another dog, did I?"

The stranger politely informed me, "I just talked with your husband, and he told me to see you about dog sitting my three dogs."

Relieved that I had not accepted another dog, I replied, "Is this Golden Retriever you have on leash one of your dogs?"

The stranger introduced himself and told me his name was Paul. We began talking when, out of the corner of my eye, I saw Zora heading for the street. I was totally shocked as last I knew Zora was safe and secure in our fenced back yard. I yelled at the top of my lungs, "Zora, come back NOW! Come here!"

Zora looked at me as if to say, "No way! Why should I?"

Then Zora spotted Paul's Golden Retriever and decided to check out this new dog. Luck was on my side. The Golden Retriever was just the bait we needed to lure Zora to us. As Zora approached and was in arm's length, I grabbed her by the collar and dragged her inside.

Then I Turned to the stranger and asked, "I am curious to know if my husband left the back gate open. Do you mind if we go have a peek?"

"Lady, evidently you don't know much about Boxers. They are great escape artists and great jumpers."

The gate was closed. I was mystified and wondered how the heck Zora managed to get out of the back yard. Paul smugly laughed as he said, "Lady, evidently you don't know much about Boxers. They are great escape artists and great jumpers. It is easy to see Zora jumped the fence. For a boxer like Zora, your fence is a joke. After all, it is only four feet tall."

Raymond returned. Within the hour we were in the back yard adding height to the fence. The extra boards may have looked funny added to the fence, but we didn't care. We would show Zora that we were in charge. Raymond and I wanted Zora to know, "You are the one at the end of the leash—not us!"

I dare say that this did not put a finish to our challenges with Zora. There were many more incidents that took place between Zora and us. One rather hilarious incident was between Zora and me. Zora was frequently barking, and with neighbors we simply could not allow excessive barking. Determined to put a stop to her barking, I went to the dollar store and purchased a squirt bottle. I filled the bottle with water. Then when Zora started barking at the back door, I opened the door and gave her a generous squirt of water. After the first time and surprise, Zora simply looked at me as if to say, "This is silly, a little water won't stop me—you silly lady."

Raymond and I were feeling trapped and desperate because we could not leave our home together. We believed that if left alone inside, Zora would tear our home to pieces; and if left alone outside, she would bark and disturb neighbors. As a solution, Raymond and I decided to purchase a bark collar that emits a slight electric shock to stop the dog from barking. The first collar was a joke. After spending many hours trying to put it together, we decided one would need a PhD in engineering to assemble the stupid thing. Determined to succeed, we went to the pet store and purchased a second collar that was rated as being highly effective. With considerable effort, Raymond assembled the new collar. With this new collar, when Zora barked we were to use a remote control device to emit a high piercing sound that would stop her from barking.

We tried to make the bark collar work, honestly we did. The trouble is that to make the collar work we had to watch Zora and activate the remote control device the second she started barking. It was winter, bitter cold outside, and neither one of us was willing to sit outside for hours waiting for Zora to bark. After all, we are Senior Citizens and sitting out in the cold waiting for a dog to bark was not our idea of fun.

As a clever option to waiting outside, we decided to watch Zora through the small window of our back door. Unfortunately, when we looked out the window, Zora spotted us and turned around positioning herself to beg to come inside. She did not even bark for us.

Zora was a fast learner. Very quickly she learned that when she saw the remote control, this was her cue not to bark. Perhaps more hilarious, Zora would jump up on our back picnic table, or perhaps on our outside upright deep freezer, and stare at us through the kitchen windows. With her beady eyes staring right at us she begged, "When can I come in? I know you can read my mind, so please respond!" Most often I would take pity on this hilarious character and succumb to her request. When Zora saw me cooking meat, she would up the ante by whining and barking until I couldn't stand it. Most often I would give up, let her in and appease her with a piece of meat.

> *I thought to myself, "I am at the end of Zora's leash, and she is having fun calling the shots."*

As I reflected upon what was happening, it seemed to me the tables had been turned. Zora was doing a fine job training me. I thought to myself, "I am at the end of Zora's leash, and she is having fun calling the shots."

Much as Zora trained us to play and listen to her, in my heart I like to believe that we also trained Zora. By the time she left us, Zora was civil to our company, would gently lay her precious head on my lap, and when playing tug-of-war with Raymond would stop when Raymond commanded her to stop. "Perhaps best of all," Raymond sighed, "Zora no longer pulled when I walked her."

When Cole returned to Victoria, we drove Zora to his house. Within minutes dog and master were playing and re-bonding. Even though their reunion was fantastic, Zora did say good-bye to us by licking us with her big sandpaper tongue. Zora was telling us she loved us, and appreciated her high spirited stay at our Doggie Palace.

Arriving back at our own casa, Raymond and I were glad to relax. Sipping our herbal granny tea, we shared how thankful we were to have enjoyed such a wild, adventuresome experience with Zora.

You know, dogs are great. Dogs live in the moment, and are a delight just the way they are *right here and right now!* No wonder we love Zora.

No wonder all dog lovers adore dogs! We feed the fur balls, they walk us, and we pick up their poo. Dogs train us, and we like to believe we have them at the end of the leash. Perhaps it is true:

"We humans think we are boss, while dogs know they are the boss."

What do you think? What is your opinion?

Who's at the end of the leash?

Secrets from a Wise Old Dog

Kobi is a sixteen year old miniature poodle and a Regal Queen. Looking at her pretty fluffy gray fur and her Royal stance, you would never guess that Kobi is sixteen. So, what is Kobi's secret to longevity, and how does she get along with other dogs in our Dog House?

Kobi's secrets for longevity and Queenship are profound. If you are a dog lover, maybe you can guess some of Kobi's secrets. They are precious secrets from a *wise old dog*! Kobi wants me to share her secrets with you. As I present them to you, they will be from Kobi's point of view as she whispered them to me via her own dog language and gestures. Here they are.

Secret One (From Kobi's Point of View):

When choosing who your human parents will be, we dogs choose well. We can do this by virtue of invoking the DOG'S LAW OF ATTRACTION. Simply put, this law of Mind and "How-Dogs-Think" puts the good thoughts of dogs into action.

Here is how the DOG'S LAW OF ATTRACTION works. When I decide that I deserve good human servants who will love and take care of me, and when I picture this absolutely and positively, magic happens. Automatically my thoughts and mental pictures are called into Being. Magically, *Good Masters* will show up for me.

In my case, I made an excellent choice with my Mom and Dad, Laurette and Lorne. They possess big hearts, good organizational skills, and they know how to stay focused until they get the best for me. These important attributes are born out of their love of dogs, their executive skills, and their determination. Laurette and Lorne knew that when they accepted their ideal dog (that's me) into their home, they were making a life-long commitment. They committed to making sure I would be happy and nurtured until my very end.

Secret Two (From Kobi's Point of View):

Once you, as a dog, have attracted good masters into your life, your next challenge is to create a loving bond with your masters—your new human parents. Good bonding includes creating the glue that inspires your masters to be totally loyal and attentive to you. You know when this has been accomplished when you can see for yourself that: (1) as their pet you are being pampered, (2) as their pet your needs are well looked after, and (3) as their pet you elicit smiles, giggles and praise from your new parents as you perform your doggie duties.

I was appropriately dressed like a queen.

In my case, I was definitely pampered. You could tell this from the get-go. I had the prettiest, most comfortable and most expensive harness of all the dogs. It had Velcro and snapped easily around the neck and belly and looked lavishly exquisite. I was appropriately dressed like a queen.

As far as my needs being looked after, my parents were meticulous as they brought their organizational and executive skills into action. As an example, before consenting to let Blenda and Raymond dog sit me, my human parents conducted a thorough interview with these prospective dog sitters. As part of the interview, they made sure that while I would be at their home, there would be no sick dogs with Kennel Cough. They also made Blenda and Raymond promise that if there were any other dogs present, that they would be compatible. In order to be compatible, the other dogs needed to be respectful of elderly dogs. The only way the future dog sitters could determine this was by intuition and intimately knowing any other dogs that would be at their home.

...from Master/Servant, Blenda's point of view.

I, Master/Servant of the Dog-House, did not have a question on my doggie intake questionnaire about the health of dogs. Because of this, I frequently had to ask the dog owners, who had dogs staying during Kobi's visit, if they were healthy and free of Kennel Cough. I must have done okay because there has never been a sick dog in my husband's and my charge while Kobi has been visiting us.

As for Kobi providing pleasure for her parents, I got the distinct impression that this happened by Kobi simply being herself. Being smart, Kobi depended upon her parents to make sure that if her feet were hurting, for instance, that they would put on her booties when she went outside. As if I could read thoughts, and I believe I can when it comes to dogs, I witnessed Kobi frequently telling her Mom and Dad that she loved them for attending to her feet and other physical needs. She affectionately showed Laurette and Lorne she felt good when they were nearby and caring for her. In her own subtle way, Kobi gave her parents so much affection that she inspired them to give her two or three walks per day. Getting two to three walks is a heck of a lot of attention and much more than many kids get—of course, this is in my humble opinion.

Secret Three (From Kobi's Point of View):

I thought, "I am an elderly dog and quite fragile, so to be safe and continue to be treated like a Queen, I am going to ASK FOR WHAT I WANT, and DEMAND THAT I GET WHAT I WANT!"

Ask for WHAT YOU WANT! Heck, I knew that when my parents left me for dog sitting, the only way I could make my stay comfortable was to ask for what I wanted. I thought, "I am an elderly dog and quite fragile, so to be safe and continue to be treated like a Queen, I am going to ASK FOR WHAT I WANT, and DEMAND THAT I GET WHAT I WANT!"

How I accomplished this was uniquely expressive. If any dog seemed overactive, like they might bump into me, I would either go find a safe place in the corner of the room or go hide out in the bedroom. If I chose the second option and any other dog came into the bedroom to pester me, I would tell Blenda or Raymond. I

46

persuaded them to either close the door so I could enjoy some privacy, or to discipline the disruptive dog.

When going on walks, I expressed what I wanted loud and clear. I would allow other gentle dogs to go along on a walk with me as long as they were on a separate leash. If the other dogs were young and too playful, before leaving I would dig my heels into the dog sitter's carpet and refuse the company of the other dog(s). I knew what was best for me, and absolutely made sure my needs were attended to. After all, I am a Queen!

… from Master/Servant, Blenda's point of view.

Once out on her walk, Kobi would set the pace. Normally I set the pace, but in her case Kobi would put up with no such nonsense. After all, Kobi admonished me, "I am Senior Top Dog and Royalty." For sure, Kobi is a Queen. If I tried yanking Kobi to hurry and she wasn't in the mood, she would not budge. On the other hand, when I let Kobi set the pace, if she felt tired she would walk slowly. Most of the time, however, Kobi felt great and would walk sprightly with the most regal prance one could imagine. If I did not know Kobi was an elder, the way she pranced I would believe she was young and a *royal princess* (not a Royal Queen). Kobi looked and acted like a *royal princess* prancing around her royal terrain. I have provided a picture of Kobi with the swans in the Esquimalt Lagoon. I love this picture because in this lagoon setting Kobi reminds me of a princess escorted by her royal swans as in Tchaikovsky's Swan Lake ballet.

Needless to say, my husband and I love Kobi and most deeply respect her for her precious secrets to longevity. For myself, enjoying a human experience and being a "Respected Senior," Kobi has taught me the following secrets for longevity:

1. Invoke the Law of Attraction and put my good thoughts into action.
2. Create a loving bond with people I care about, and who in return will care about me.
3. ASK FOR WHAT I WANT, and DEMAND THAT I GET WHAT I WANT.

Whether we are young, middle age, or seniors, I believe we can all learn a great deal from a *wise old dog* like Kobi. What is your opinion?

Scruffy the Messenger

It was 10am on the morning of June 6, 2013 when the phone rang and a bright and cheerful voice greeted me. Sean Hendricks wanted to know if I would dog sit Scruffy, his three year old male Shih Tzu/Jack Russell dog, for approximately three weeks starting tomorrow. Sean was a Navy man who was being transferred from Winnipeg to Victoria, BC, Canada. He needed someone to dog sit Scruffy while he moved his household belongings to the coast, to Victoria, BC.

There was urgency in Sean's voice. I quite liked him as he had a friendly commanding ring to his voice. Intuitively taking a shine to Sean, I replied, "I would love to dog sit Scruffy; however, the only way I could do this would be to take him on a week-long trip. My husband and I are planning on going to the Interior of BC, the Okanagan Valley. If you agree, we will take Scruffy, that is, providing we first meet him and like him."

Sean replied, "That would be great. My dog is my best friend, and it is important that I have special people to dog sit him. Your ad in Used Victoria told me that you and your husband are perfect. If it is okay with you, I will come over right away."

Sean meant what he said. Ten minutes later Sean arrived. He caught my husband and me in the middle of eating breakfast. Raymond asked Sean if he could come back in twenty minutes. Sean, being a dynamic young gentleman, replied, "That would be fine. I will go walk Scruffy at the Goldstream Park and be back in twenty minutes."

Exactly twenty minutes later, Sean was knocking at our back door. All other people who have wanted dog sitting have come to the front door, so the fact that Sean insisted on coming through the back yard to our back porch entrance convinced me that he was uniquely different. I wondered if his dog was also going to prove different. Well, now that breakfast was finished, I had an opportunity to take a real good look at Scruffy.

As I examined this dog with his scruffy white fur laced with golden streaks and saw the twinkle in his eyes, it was easy to fall in love him. Scruffy showed himself to be an attentive dog. He carefully listened to his dad doing exactly what he asked. For example, when his dad asked him to sit, Scruffy sat. Sean treated Scruffy like his best friend and buddy. Perhaps that is why his dad affectionately called Scruffy his "Little Man".

Sean signed the intake papers and gave us written permission to take Scruffy with us, including participating in the workshop we were attending in Armstrong, BC. Armstrong is right next to Vernon in the Okanagan Valley, BC. The workshop was on Intercellular Communication, and the purpose of the workshop was to teach the participants how to communicate more effectively with dogs, horses and even with humans. Part of the agenda included scanning the bodies of the dogs we had brought with us. Using this procedure, we discovered what was happening in their bodies. For example, we learned if there was any physical disturbance. We also learned to intuitively become aware of anything that the dog would like to communicate to his/her master.

Now let's return to talking about Sean and his dog. The next day about the same time, 9am, there was a loud knock at the back door. Sean was standing there facing me with Scruffy. Sean threw a few sticks for Scruffy, playing with him one last time. He bent down and looking into Scruffy's eyes affectionately told his buddy, "Be a good Little Man. I will be back soon." With these departing words, Sean turned around so he was no longer facing Scruffy and quickly walked away.

When Scruffy came through the back door into our kitchen, he discovered Rascal, a little miniature Dachshund that we were dog sitting. Immediately the two dogs began sniffing one another—checking each other out. Rascal is an eight month old pup who loves to play and be joyful. Fulfilling his purpose of bringing joy to other dog by being playful, Rascal went up to Scruffy and began gently nipping at his neck until Scruffy got annoyed and started chasing Rascal. Together they raced non-stop round the house until, making far too much racket, I put them outside in the back yard. There they continued their play with Rascal often humping Scruffy and vice versa. In their doggie world, it didn't seem to matter that they were both male dogs. I believe they were merely into the humping for the physical contact.

Raymond and I were relieved both dogs were having so much fun playing together. Knowing they were taken care of, we could spend our time packing and tidying up the house before leaving the next day. We planned on taking Scruffy with us on our trip and leaving Rascal with another dog sitter. The dogs would be separated and undergo a lot of sudden change. I was only mildly confident they could handle the disruptive changes. Awakening early the next morning, Raymond and I delivered Rascal to our dear friend and back-up dog sitter.

Our friend was concerned when she saw Rascal. She feared that due to his small size he would be able to duck under her fence and escape. Also, she did not like the collar Rascal was wearing. After clearly stating her objections, our friend acquiesced and said she would do her best. Rascal cried when we left, and I felt so bad—so guilty. I felt as if I was abandoning this darling little puppy when he had just been with us a couple of weeks and needed our emotional support.

I silently pondered, "But what can I do? I can't think of anything to do differently. I feel compelled to attend this workshop, and I know darn well Rascal can't join us because he isn't house broken and is far too yappy. I will simply have to trust that Rascal will be okay. Mentally I'll surround Rascal and the dog sitter with white, protective light."

Enough about Rascal. Our friend, Dwight Whitson, arrived at our friend's home in his car. Raymond and I quickly got in our car and followed Dwight to a safe place where we parked our car before boarding the Ferry taking us to the Vancouver mainland. Since we were being picked up in Tsawwassen, where the ferry docks, we boarded the ferry as foot passengers.

Being foot passengers and taking a dog with us on the ferry proved to be an interesting experience. Scruffy seemed to know that it was important to relieve himself physically before stepping onto the ferry, so he pooed and peed like a good little boy outside the ferry and close to the entrance. When Scruffy was finished pooing and peeing, we walked onto the vessel. Once onboard, we were directed to the Pet Room that was below decks, down where cars and busses are housed. The Pet Room was small and had a nauseating effect with the rancid reek of urine (most unpleasant). In spite of the unpleasant stench, we pet lovers found lots to talk about including many stories to share. Scruffy was in his glory: alive, alert, and playful. Time passed quickly.

Once off the ferry, we were picked up by a friend who drove us to Chilliwack, about a two hour drive. Chilliwack is located in the outskirts of the Fraser Valley, right before you ascend up the big mountains to Hope. In Chilliwack we spent the night with Bette who is Raymond's sister. Bette's condo does not allow dogs, so we put a towel over Scruffy's head to camouflage him as we snuck him into the Condo. Scruffy seemed to know what he was supposed to do and co-operated by keeping his head low—safely concealed underneath the towel. Once inside the Condo, Raymond's two little Nephews wanted to play with this cute little fur ball.

Scruffy was very cautious. He did not want to be treated like a little play toy, and unfortunately that is the way little children often treat dogs.

When we finally arrived in Vernon, BC, we stayed at a B & B where there was another dog. Again, Scruffy got along well. The following night, however, was a different story. We were invited to stay at a lady-friend's home while she was away camping. Here we met with some challenges. Our friend owned a cat, and it was inside the house. Upon meeting, Scruffy and the cat were instantly at each other's throats. I yelled at them to stop, but neither of them would back down. I stood frozen with fear. Thank goodness Raymond was present. He came to the rescue. Raymond bravely swooped down and separated Scruffy from the cat. After this frightening experience, we made sure Scruffy and the cat each had their own territory. As if this wasn't enough for me to deal with, the Universe delivered still another upsetting experience.

I was upstairs at the top of the landing of the stairs, and I noticed a pile of cat poo in the middle of the rug. After some investigation, I got the picture. Dear sweet Scruffy was taking some of the cat poo from the litter box and eating it. I thought, "God, how awful. So this is why Scruffy isn't eating the dry dog food that Sean left with us. He doesn't like his own food and, in fact, prefers cat poo. I will have to do something about this."

With no car at my disposal to run to the store, my only option was to wait until the next day to buy Scruffy a different brand of dog food—hopefully a brand that

Scruffy would eat. Although I thought Scruffy's eating cat poo was disgusting, I later discovered when reading up on dogs that are vomiting that young puppies often raid cat litter boxes.

Being the only dog in the crowd that wouldn't settle down, I was thoroughly embarrassed.

Finally, Monday arrived. This was the first day of the workshop. In attendance were eighteen people and about nine dogs. The workshop took place in a barn that had been converted into an inviting workshop space. As participants, we were asked to sit on chairs with a leash for our dog and a rug for him/her to lie upon. All the dogs obeyed and became quiet—that is, all the dogs except Scruffy. Scruffy started whining and whimpering in an attempt to get loose. Being the only dog in the crowd that wouldn't settle down, I was thoroughly embarrassed. Scruffy's behavior was extremely disruptive. Acting rather desperate, Scruffy jumped into Susan's lap. Susan was sitting next to me. Susan had no dog with her; however, she had owned dogs and evidently was very good with them. She looked into Scruffy's eyes and seemed to be reassuring Scruffy that everything was okay. After A few minutes with Susan, Scruffy slowly walked over to the gentleman sitting next to her and looked intensely into his eyes, as if communicating an important message to him. Susan said that this was one of the main reasons why Scruffy was attending—to deliver this message that was of vital importance. After the message was delivered, Scruffy returned and settled down on the rug at my feet.

During the course of the workshop, this same scenario repeated itself numerous times. Each time it would end with Scruffy going to the gentleman to once again deliver his message.

Later I asked Susan what she did to communicate so effectively with Scruffy. She responded, "My only secret is that I am good at communicating with dogs."

I replied, "I guess so!!!"

Susan followed up by adding, "You know, Scruffy wants to be your dog—to live with you and Raymond. Somehow Scruffy will end up being your dog."

Susan's news was exciting and disturbing at the same time. If this really happened, because I liked Scruffy so much, I believe we would find a way to keep him. For the life of me, however, I could not imagine Scruffy's Dad wanting to give up his "Little Man." For this to happen, I figured something tragic would have to occur. Susan calmed me down as she said, "Don't worry. I feel assured that somehow Scruffy would become your dog."

As I opened my heart, I felt totally wonderful, loving, and at peace.

For the very first time since I started dog sitting, I gave myself permission to fully open my heart to love, and to accept Scruffy. I did this believing Scruffy could end up being our very own dog. As I opened my heart, I felt totally wonderful, loving, and at peace. At the same time, remembering how much Scruffy's human Dad loved him, I reminded myself that Scruffy had such a wonderful Dad that I was, indeed, honored to be able to take good care of Scruffy.

What happened a few days later at the workshop was another shocker. Scruffy transitioned into becoming a therapy dog for Raymond. This began when our workshop leader, Loesje Jacob, began working with Raymond doing some human intercellular communication. I now include this thrilling description as I wrote after the workshop to be included in the author's corner of the *QUANTUM LOVE GENE* website (www.quantumlovegene.com).

If you choose to read what I wrote, please read it with an open mind and heart. If what happened sounds ridiculous, then just leave it at that: ridiculous and absurd. On the other hand, if you do like what happened, then you will sense how profound and tuned in Scruffy truly is. An excerpt from my description follows:

The date is June 12, 2013. It is the third day of the Linking Awareness Intercellular Workshop presented by Loesje Jacob in Armstrong, BC, located in the Okanagan Valley of British Columbia, Canada. There were seventeen of us humans attending the workshop and eight to ten dogs. We sat in a large semi-circle in the barn that had been converted into workshop space. We had been doing awesome work through guided meditations. As part of the meditations we entered into an intuitive process in which we mentally scanned the bodies of live dogs and horses to determine where there were health issues and what the animals wanted to communicate to us humans. In the case of the dogs we scanned, they usually had something special to communicate to their owners.

Having successfully participated in this workshop for a couple of days, my husband, Raymond, asked our wonderful facilitator, Loesje, if she was going to do any work with humans. About ten minutes later Loesje answered Raymond by saying (and I am paraphrasing), "Clear the massage table. Raymond, I want you up on the massage table."

Loesje's message was clear. Raymond laid himself down and asked Loesje, "Is it okay if I go into Theta?" By that, Raymond literally was asking Loesje if it was okay for him to enter into a hypnogogic state that is used in hypnosis—in this case, in self-induced hypnosis.

Loesje responded in the affirmative. Raymond took one deep breath and was gone. No longer was he consciously aware of the proceedings around him.

Sensing the change, this little three year old male Shih Tzu/Jack Russell dog, Scruffy, that we had started dog sitting just five days prior, started making a terrible fuss. He was on-leash, sitting in front of my chair, on the floor. The rest of the dogs were quiet. Scruffy broke the dog silence with a piercing howl. All heads turned to look at Scruffy. Loesje said, "Let Scruffy off the leash. Let him go."

Scruffy got right into the licking and Loesje told us that Scruffy was part of healing.

Scruffy dashed over to the massage table trying to find a way to climb up on it. Loesje lifted Scruffy up and placed him at Raymond's feet. This was not good enough for Scruffy. He inched his way along the edge of the massage table up to the front of Raymond's head. Scruffy then began licking Raymond all over his head— and I literally mean all over his head. Raymond didn't move an inch and normally Raymond only tolerates a little licking by dogs. Scruffy got right into the licking, and Loesje told us that Scruffy was part of healing. Scruffy was on a new mission.

When "Enough licking was enough", Loesje lifted Scruffy down and handed him to Dwight Whitson who had accompanied Raymond and me to Armstrong. Somewhat reluctantly, Scruffy followed Dwight, but all the while keeping his eyes glued to what was happening with Raymond.

Back at the massage table, Loesje rubbed gently over Raymond's stomach area. Perhaps soothed by her gentle strokes, Raymond started talking. Actually, what really happened is that Raymond started commanding us in a loud and powerful voice that was different from his normal voice: "Awaken! Awaken! The time has come. You must awaken! Awaken and know that you are Spiritual Light Beings! The time has come. It is important to hurry. The Black Hole is approaching faster than anticipated."

Then Raymond became silent. The room was so quiet you could hear a pin drop. All of us were taking in his words—the powerful commands. It was obvious to most sitting in the room that these were not Raymond's commands. They were commands channeled by an Alien Being through Raymond. This Alien Being was Angelica from Pleiades—the same Angelica who delivered her message for the world through forty one consecutive dreams of Raymond's.

With the channeling complete, Loesje moved her hands in little circular movements above Raymond's left temple. With those types of finger-hand movements, it looked like the same movements one makes when kneading bread—only this time Loesje was kneading the energy Raymond needed. Loesje spoke. She said, "Now I know why the Pleiadians chose Raymond to be the messenger. Raymond is wired differently! I will make some necessary adjustments to keep the communication portal open."

I interpreted Loesje's words to mean she was making sure that Raymond's portal for receiving information from Angelica and other Pleiadians would be kept open. Loesje believes in the importance of Angelica's message for the Planet, and wants it to be delivered.

Loesje ended by saying, "I commit to helping Raymond and keeping the portal open."

When Raymond awakened he had no memory of anything that happened—absolutely no memory of the dog licking his face, of what he said in his commanding voice, or anything that Loesje said or did. The last thing Raymond remembered was asking if it would be okay to go into Theta.

Now, back to the story:

Strange, the longer Raymond and I had Scruffy as our companion on our trip, the more he grew on me. I began to feel like Scruffy was an extension of myself. I sensed we were a lot alike. Scruffy and I both liked people and did our best to make them happy. Whomever we visited, Scruffy was kind to them. When we visited my brother after the workshop, Scruffy befriended my brother's dog named Charlie, and Charlie stood outside our bedroom door at night waiting for Scruffy to come out and play. Scruffy was just so darn cute and well behaved. It really is quite amazing, but the very first week that we had Scruffy I was able to trust him and take him off-leash. Whether I called him by using my thoughts or by my voice, Scruffy was quick to respond and do what I asked. This, of course, added to my belief that Scruffy was an invisible extension of me.

Days passed rapidly on our trip, and before we knew it, Raymond and I were back in Victoria. I was dreading picking up Rascal from our friend, the dog sitter. When we arrived, I could hear Rascal barking and thought I would be lucky if he would talk to us.

Oh! Was I ever wrong. Rascal jumped all over me greeting me with kisses. Evidently he had a fantastic time winning the hearts of my girlfriend and her friends. Now, however, he was ready to return home. I wondered if he would be jealous of Scruffy—I suspected he would.

Once again, I was wrong. Rascal was not jealous. Scruffy was not protective. The truth is that both dogs were delighted to see each another again, and within minutes were playing. Once back at our home, Scruffy was friendly to all the dogs that came for dog sitting. I felt so blessed to have Scruffy around. For me personally, Scruffy also had a message, only I wasn't quite sure what it was. I wondered if it might be that he was going to somehow become our dog. I knew if he were to become our dog that I would be ecstatic. As one friend pointed out, "Scruffy would never win awards as a show dog because he has what they call an overbite." An overbite occurs when your lower jaw protrudes out a bit beyond the upper jaw. Even though Scruffy has an overbite, I didn't care. To me Scruffy was simply a perfect dog. I knew I would be blessed if this very special dog became mine.

Secretly wanting Scruffy, but realistically knowing that Scruffy had a wonderful Dad who loved him and couldn't wait to see him, I knew I had to stay prepared for the day Scruffy might leave me. I decided to call Scruffy's dad and see how his move was progressing.

Sean said he was tired but that the move was progressing well and he would be back in about a week. I told Sean that Raymond and I had become quite attached to Scruffy, and since Sean was in the Navy we would love to dog sit for him when he went away—or maybe during the days when he was at work. Sean said he would sit down with us over coffee when he returned.

"Well," I thought to myself, "Perhaps we won't own Scruffy, but we could take care of him often. That could be satisfying to us, to Sean, and to Scruffy."

On the walks with Scruffy I made a conscious decision to enjoy every single moment

On the walks with Scruffy I made a conscious decision to enjoy every single moment, thus savoring the flavor of such an exquisite dog. It was so much fun while walking the dogs to see Scruffy play with the Golden Retriever, Carly, and with Lacee, who is the Chihuahua. All three dogs had earned the privilege of being off leash, so they were able to run and chase freely. It was a good exercise for me to make a conscious decision to enjoy every moment. This way I would more thoroughly enjoy these unique and rare cherished moments, and also be able to store them in my memory-bank.

A couple of days later, I had just finished breakfast and was sitting down at my computer, when I looked at

Scruffy who had taken his position on the blanket next to my feet. I opened my heart wide and sent him love. I decided it was time to tell Scruffy that his Dad would soon be returning. I carefully created a mental image of Scruffy's human Dad returning home and mentally projected the image into Scruffy's mind.

Much to my utter shock, within five minutes of my projecting the image into Scruffy's mind, there was a loud knock at the back door. The door is about six feet from my computer where I was sitting. I looked up and through the window in the door I saw Sean. Logic told me that my only choice that made sense was to open the door and welcome him.

Sean grinned and apologized saying, "I have come to pick up Scruffy and would have called you first, but lost your phone number. We made good time on our trip, and I am back a few days earlier than anticipated."

Sean opened his arms so Scruffy could jump up on him. At first Scruffy looked a bit confused. Then Sean leaned down and said to Scruffy, "Little Man, come to Dad. I missed you."

With these words, Scruffy jumped into his Dad's arms. The conversion went quickly. Scruffy knew his Dad, where he belonged, and his sacred buddy who he had loved for so many years.

I told the tears in my tender heart that this was a great opportunity for me to practice unconditional love. I said to myself, "For love to be unconditional, I must be willing and happy for Scruffy to return to such a wonderful Dad – a Dad who loves him very, very much."

Needing to encourage myself further, I spoke to my heart saying, "I can do it! I can replace those tears in my heart with a warm and cozy spot reserved just for Scruffy."

With these words that I secretly spoke to my aching heart, I felt my heart grow warm. Once again I knew I would be safe from heart-wrenching grief.

Before Sean departed, we sat down and shared. Sean said that if he ever needed a dog sitter he would be sure to use us. Meanwhile, on a daily basis he would be leaving Scruffy at home while he worked. He also planned on getting another dog, a Jack Russell, to keep Scruffy company.

I agreed with Sean that having a second dog to keep Scruffy company would be a good idea. When settled in their new home Sean promised to bring Scruffy over for a visit.

Finally it was time for Scruffy to leave. Scruffy did give Raymond and me a big hug and kiss. Then Sean departed out the back gate saying to Scruffy, "Come on Little Man. The car is waiting for you!"

As Scruffy jumped into the back seat of the car, hot tears were rolling down my cheeks. Even though I had just talked to myself consoling my heart, I could not control my tears. The big *Brave Me* was glad for Scruffy. The emotional *Mother-in-me* was feeling devastated to see my baby depart. Yes, my heart ached. Because I was having an emotional human experience, I decided to let the experience happen and know that eventually I would come out the other side to victory. As a result of my experience with Scruffy and his dad, I would be even stronger in my capacity to extend unconditional love.

After an hour my tears abated. During the week after Scruffy departed, there was a huge empty feeling in the house—like something dear and essential was missing. Rascal seemed to sense our loss and was far more attentive to both Raymond and me. Toward the end of the week, Raymond and I went to the movies a couple of times to get our minds off of missing him and into being grateful that Scruffy had such a wonderful loving Dad.

As is often said, "Time heals." In this case, with the passage of time we grew increasingly thankful that Scruffy has such a loving home, and that we were privileged to have been a part of his life—to receive the lessons he gave us on opening ourselves up to true unconditional love.

"Love knows no boundaries."

As I am writing this story, it is approximately a month since Scruffy left. I called his Dad and he said he would like to bring Scruffy over next week end for a visit. This will be a challenge, since I want to see Scruffy and yet not be possessive. The good news is that I am up for the challenge. "Love knows no boundaries."

PS: I am working on the editing for my dog story memories and it is two months since Raymond and I had the pleasure of dog-sitting Scruffy.

When Raymond and I opened our hearts fully to Scruffy, we got to experience a deeper love, the increased intuitive communication between dog and man/woman, and a deeper level of compassion and respect.

This morning I got a big WOW! A big WOW is when I get hit over the head with a sudden Truth. I realized that the gift Scruffy gave us continues to grow. When Raymond and I opened our hearts fully to Scruffy, we got to experience a deeper love, an increased intuitive communication between dog and man/woman, and a deeper level of compassion and respect. Having received this gift, our hearts continue to grow more open and receptive. As a result, dog owners are noticing how happy their dogs are visiting with us. We are observing how easy it is to communicate with the dogs, to hold them in our arms and love them, and to gently let the dogs know that while we love them we respect their loving bond with their owners.

In closing, I want to officially thank Scruffy for his gift of unconditional love. I also want to thank all dogs for being so patient with us while we learn from the secrets they graciously share with us.

Rascal the Alien Dog

Melissa and her partner, Jonathan, wanted a reliable dog sitter. They were well-to-do energetic students attending a local University. Jonathan was from Taiwan, and Melissa from Malaysia. They met on campus and fell in love. Looking at the kindness in Melissa's face, I detected a strong Mother instinct, and concluded that is why they decided to get a dog for their very own.

> *He looked like a little Alien with his long floppy ears, big saucer like inquisitive eyes, and sleek long body that was only a few inches off the ground.*

What a choice for a dog! When Melissa and Jonathan knocked on the front door, Melissa was carrying Rascal in her arms. He looked like a little Alien with his long floppy ears, big saucer like inquisitive eyes, and sleek long body that was only a few inches off the ground. In truth, this small Alien dog looked so small, unusual and cuddly that he warmed both your heart and giggle factor. As an eight month old puppy, it didn't take long until Rascal had squirmed loose from Melissa's arms and began frantically dashing around the room exploring his new surroundings. In case you haven't already guessed, Rascal is a Miniature Dachshund who is full of life.

As Cesar Milan recommends, when you meet a new dog, you should let the dog come to you on the dog's own terms. Taking his advice, I patiently waited for Rascal to come to me. I waited and waited, but my patience didn't work. Rascal would not come. Raymond, my husband, tried to reach out to Rascal and all that accomplished was Rascal's running away from Raymond with his tail between his legs. Finally we came to the brilliant conclusion that Rascal was skittish. Melissa called Rascal shy.

Even though Rascal would not come to us, Raymond and I were confident that with time we would win Rascal over. We believed it would be a growing experience to have this wiggly little Dachshund with us for two and a half months while his parents were traveling abroad. Melissa and Jonathan wanted us as dog sitters, and we wanted to dog sit Rascal. The only obstacle standing in our way was agreeing upon a price. Jonathan was young, majoring in finance, and I believe from a family whose natural way was to negotiate until they got a very good deal. Raymond and I sensed this and were prepared for some good ol' negotiating. We haggled and finally settled on a price that was only slightly less than the price we thought we would agree upon. The final outcome was that we struck a good deal –Jonathan was happy and so were we. We were both winners.

After we had agreed upon a price, Jonathan then took out from his bag what looked like diapers. He explained that we would need to keep a diaper out on the floor as Rascal was not yet housebroken.

"WHOOPIE!" I thought, "This is just what I need".

Raymond was beside himself and said, "If we are taking a dog that is not yet housebroken, it will be Blenda's responsibility to pick up after the dog. I hope she will charge extra for house training."

For our next surprise, Jonathan and Melissa pointed out that Rascal was not yet fixed. Jonathan went on to explain, "Rascal might get a little sexually excited or anxious and could even emit a horrific smelling odor called a pheromone." Of course, with Rascal not being fixed, this meant that I would have to watch and make sure that there were no female dogs in season staying with us at our home. Raymond laughed because for such a little Alien guy, Rascal had two large "you know whats".

Just looking at Rascal, you knew he was a real character.

Yes, Rascal was quite a sight with his long flappy ears, big overgrown snout, long body low-to-the-ground, and his two large "you know whats". Weirder than fiction, this Dachshund was so funny looking that he was adorable. Just looking at Rascal, you knew he was a real character.

Finally getting us to consent to all the wonderful attributes of Rascal, especially housetraining him, our young and happy couple departed quickly while they were still ahead. They left saying they would be back in two days when they were departing on their trip. They would drop off Rascal then.

Two days after their initial intake interview, the doorbell rang. Rascal arrived. Jonathan was carrying a huge big box of diaper pads. Looking at the gigantic box of diapers, I felt completely overwhelmed. Sensing my anxiety, Jonathan assured me that it would all work out. I can't say that I believed Jonathan or that his kind words helped, yet, I was thankful we shared a good working relationship.

Jonathan's wife, Melissa, helped by changing the subject. Melissa said she was sorry that she had forgotten Rascal's leash. I assured Melissa this would be okay as I had many leashes. They had no bed for Rascal so I assured Melissa we could use our spare doggie bed.

Finally Jonathan and Melissa said good bye. The front door closed, and I managed to lift Rascal into my arms so I could hold him up to the living room window and he could see his Mom and Dad leaving. Jonathan and Melissa drove off. Now Raymond and I had Rascal all to ourselves.

To put the dog at ease and win some brownie points, I thought I would be real smart and take Rascal out for a walk. Truthfully, I also was hopeful Rascal would do his business outside rather than inside the house. Because I had two other dogs in addition to Rascal, I put Rascal on a third leash. When all dogs were securely on their leashes, I headed outside. I closed the front door and was walking across the front lawn when suddenly Rascal yanked himself loose from his collar and started racing toward the street.

Shocked and scared stiff, I yelled, "RASCAL, come back! Come back right now Rascal!"

RASCAL had deaf ears. He ran out into the middle of the street. Terrified, I ran after Rascal. I had visions of his running away or getting run over by a car. He was so small. I worried, "How could anyone even see Rascal?"

Rascal was hanging upside down, but at this point I didn't care how Rascal was hanging, or the fact that he was peeing all over me.

"My God!" I panicked as I saw a car approaching us. Standing in the middle of the street, I raised up my hands employing the car to stop. Perhaps more terrified than I was, Rascal started running round in circles. I bent over, and by the grace of God managed to grab him. Absolutely terrified, Rascal peed all over me including showering my face with his wet pee. Rascal was hanging upside down, but at this point I didn't care how Rascal was hanging, or the fact that he was peeing all over me. All I cared about was that I could get him off the street and returned to safety.

I must have been quite the sight with two dogs on leash and the third miniature dachshund hanging upside down being frantically carried across the street by a little old lady.

"Heck with it!" I congratulated myself, "I made it!" I managed to get the little bugger inside the house and shut the door.

Safe at last, I took a good look at Rascal's collar and

observed that it had some expandable elastic on it. I thought, "No wonder Rascal got loose. All Rascal had to do was slip his head out of the collar. This takes the cake! There will be no walks for Rascal until I get him a proper collar."

Having made this decision, I settled Rascal on the couch upstairs while I walked the other two dogs. Rascal curled up in a ball and in his own dog language said, "I agree. Because I don't want a repeat of what just happened, I prefer that I wait this one out. No thanks, I don't want to go walking with you."

When I arrived home with the other two dogs, Rascal greeted us. This was, however, all this small little fur-ball would do. Anytime I came near him, Rascal would run away as if I was the big bad monster. In a way, I understood. I thought, "The poor little guy, I sympathize with Rascal's being terrified. He just encountered this horrific street incident compounded by the fact that he probably felt sadly abandoned by his owners. After all, this is his first time being left in a strange home, and his parents are nowhere in sight."

Heck! Looking at this from a dog's point of view, let's review what happened. The first day Rascal arrives at a strange house. In the first hour in his new surroundings Rascal is brought out into yard, gets loose, and runs into the street where he becomes absolutely panicked. In response, I yell at Rascal and grab him upside down and carry him inside. What a beginning for a dog who already is squeamish. It stands to reason why this cute little fur-ball would consider me a big bad monster. All day and all night Rascal dodged me. Even his dinner didn't appeal to him. He barely ate.

I sometimes think that if we humans were willing to learn the art of forgiveness from dogs, we would enjoy far more happy relationship and far more peace in the world.

Much to my surprise, the following day Rascal sauntered over to me looking for some petting, and then begged to get up on Raymond's captain chair for some pampering. In his own dog language, Rascal was showing us that he had forgiven us. Forgiving the other person is an endearing aspect of dogs. To my knowledge, dogs rarely hold a grudge. I sometimes think that if we humans were willing to learn the art of forgiveness from dogs, we would enjoy far more happy relationships and far more peace in the world. Anyway, putting my judgments aside, I was delighted and thankful that Rascal had forgiven me.

With forgiveness out of the way, Rascal became attentive to the other dogs we were dog sitting. One of the dogs was with us for three weeks, and that dog was Scruffy. Funny, the names were both very cute, and yet the dogs came from very different parents. Scruffy came to us from a young Navy Steward who was moving to Victoria from Winnipeg and needed a home for his dog while he was away. Scruffy was a super friendly dog and so, in less than half a day, the two dogs were already buddy-bosom friends and chasing one another round the house. Not being fixed, Rascal spent much time trying to mount Scruffy. Scruffy put up with this for as long as he could, and then let out a little growl telling Rascal he had enough.

Rascal had a nasty habit of mounting almost any small or medium sized dog who came to visit. His favorite dog was Riley, the very handsome four year old Bichon Poo who is the "Doggie in the Window," and about whom I wrote that story. Rascal simply would not let Riley alone and Riley would put up with Rascal's antics with a slight grin on his face. This all went well until I noticed that Riley's halter collar looked strange. I went over to Riley and discovered that our Alien dog had chewed right through Riley's halter, and it was drooping down over his chest. I took it off and handed it to Raymond who is quite the fix-it man. Raymond found that Rascal had bitten through the collar in two places, not one. Diligently Raymond tried to mend the halter, but it simply wasn't possible. Finally we found another halter in our arsenal of supplies and adjusted it to Riley so he would be able to go for a walk with us. I really didn't want to explain what happened to his parents, but knew that I had to tell the truth. In this case, Truth was as strange as fiction. I offered to purchase Riley a new halter, but Riley's parents were most understanding and assured me that everything was okay. After this event, I knew for sure that Rascal deserved his name. He was a real Rascal and very sneaky.

Indeed, we had a real live wire on our hands. Rascal loved to run around and seemed so much in-the-moment that even though he had the diapers upon which he was to pee and poo, he frequently went on the carpet or hardwood floor. Since I had promised Raymond that I would do the cleanup, I got the honors. Being a retired minister, I believed that prayers would help and so started praying that Rascal would get the idea from the other dogs and learn that the right place to pee and poo is outside. The next week Rascal answered my prayers and pooed outside a couple of times. I was sure to reward him with lots of pets and praise.

Well, the very unfortunate part of taking Rascal is that soon after we consented that we would take him we had two things happen. We were invited to a wonderful workshop in Intercellular Communication in Armstrong, BC, that is about a twelve hour trip from our home. Also my very special brother, whom I love so much, was not feeling well. I wanted to go visit with him. He is about a five hour drive from Armstrong. Combined this would be about a ten day trip. In order to make the trip, I would have to ask my good friend, Sheila, if she would dog sit Rascal. I knew I could trust Sheila because she works with therapy dogs, has a dog of her own, and has proven her worth. Sheila agreed. With the consent of Scruffy's Dad, Raymond and I would take Scruffy with us. There was no way we could take Rascal with us as he constantly yapped and was not housebroken.

When the day arrived that I had to take Rascal to Sheila's home, he seemed happy as both he and Scruffy were in the car. When I finally had to say good bye to Rascal, he whined and looked at me with such sad eyes that it ripped my heart apart. I worried about Rascal being left twice in such a short time. The good news was that I trusted Sheila totally and knew how much she loved dogs.

Oh! I must confess, however, that I wasn't too thrilled about one thing. When I was about ready to leave Sheila's home, she said that she didn't remember my telling her that Rascal was not housebroken and would not have taken him if she had known...also she was very upset about the possibility of his sneaking through her fence and did not approve of the second-hand collar that I had purchased him. I invited Sheila to buy another collar and promised to pay for it. Having addressed Sheila's concerns, I was confident she would do an excellent job (and by the way, Sheila did do a great job and by the time Rascal left she absolutely adored him).

I am happy to report that our trip was delightful. During the trip we bonded with Scruffy. Returning home, I was concerned about how Rascal would fit back in. As per usual, my concerns were unwarranted. Dogs are so understanding and forgiving. Rascal greeted me with an abundance of licks. When Rascal jumped in the car and discovered Scruffy was waiting for him, once again the two dogs became instant friends.

Because I had bonded so thoroughly with Scruffy on the trip, I found that I wanted to favor Scruffy. This desire awarded me with some very unpleasant feelings of guilt; however, these feelings were more for my own self-inflicted, self-punishing benefit and not Rascal`s. Rascal seemed immune to my guilt feelings. You see, Rascal has this uncanny way of dispelling negativity. He is so intent on playing and making sure that all dogs and humans play whenever they can that his joyful playfulness cuts through all guilt, negativity and jealousy. This is the way Rascal expresses his love and caring. It reminds me of a little baby wanting to play and is irresistible. With other dogs Rascal will nip at their legs or neck in a playful manner until usually they decide to make good on Rascal`s invitation to have some fun. Rascal has achieved getting many dogs to play that normally would not play, including a senior citizen Lab who initially thought that Rascal was some sort of joke.

What has been absolutely precious for Raymond and me is watching Rascal play with a fifteen month old Golden Retriever, named Carly, who we dog sit three times a week. At first when Carly visited with us and Rascal started nipping at her lower legs, Carly would look at Rascal as if to say, "Who do you think you are, you little Twerp?" Even though Rascal is about an eighth of Carly's size, Carly's attitude didn't faze Rascal one bit. After several days of Rascal nipping at Carly's lower legs, Carly smiled and with a new perkiness started nuzzling Rascal as if to say, "Okay, I surrender. You may be small, but you are irresistible. I will play." Accepting the invitation, Rascal nipped and jumped up on Carly with even more vigor. Carly, in the gentlest manner, put her big paws on Rascal's back and nudged Rascal. Then Rascal found her tug-of-war rope and enticed Carly to take the other end. Together they played tug-of-war and then started chasing wildly round the house. When it got to be too much, I coerced them to go outside. The Miniature Alien Rascal and the Gentle Big Jolly Giant make quite the pair playing together.

Now that Rascal felt more at home with us, Rascal started exploring all the nooks and crannies of our home, both inside and outside. Of this we got proof. One day the doorbell rang and a neighbor said to us, "Your dog has been running up and down the street barking. If you don't take care of your dog, he will get run over."

The big question was, "How in the world did Rascal get out when the back gate was securely closed and there were no breaks in the fence?"

This small dark crawl space had to be what Rascal had discovered and used to make his get-away.

As we pondered the answer we noticed that under the back porch deck there was a long dark space that, when followed to its end, led to a little crawl space between the wall of the back deck and the ground. This small dark crawl space had to be what Rascal had discovered and used to make his get-away. We took some boards and plugged up the space Rascal used for his get-away. This worked for about three weeks until Rascal once again got restless. This time Raymond heard Rascal barking out front and discovered his escape. Raymond couldn't figure it out since the side was boarded up. I suggested that perhaps the boards were not tight enough against the ground and Rascal had snuck out. This time Raymond nailed the boards to the side of the house. We were confident this would fix Rascal once and for all.

Even though Rascal is AN ALIEN DOG and a purebred Rascal, both Raymond and I grew to love him more and more each day. Being Senior citizens, Rascal is just what the doctor ordered to give us a touch of humor and playfulness. For example, when we are eating dinner, Rascal is sure to position himself so he sits between us. He sits squarely on his fanny with his big long body tall and erect, paws circling round and round begging, and eyes looking ever so mournful and deserving. Of course Rascal is saying, "I'm so cute. How could you possibly resist me? Show some pity for a poor hungry dog."

Rascal will climb up on the dining room chair next to me and if there is room put his paws on the glass table and proceed to look so pitiful it is impossible to resist him.

Most often Raymond and I surrender and give Rascal a treat from our plate. If, however, we do not succumb to Rascal's sitting on his all-fours, Rascal will climb up on the dining room chair next to me and, if there is room, put his paws on the glass table and proceed to look so pitiful it is impossible to resist him. If there is not room between himself and the table to sit up, Rascal will make sure we can see him through the glass table. Although this is a small thing Rascal does, it is the small antics that add so much joy and laughter to our lives.

Rascal has been with us for two and a half months. We are expecting his parents to return in another couple of weeks. Although it will be very sad for us when he leaves, we are preparing ourselves by knowing how happy his parents will be to see their little companion again. They have been very gracious calling me, watching Rascal on Skype and showing their gratitude for potty training him, walking him so he is confident off-leash, curbing his continuous barking, and supporting his transformation from a shy dog to an outstanding dog. Indeed, Rascal is an outstanding dog that is a catalyst making sure the dogs who visit us have fun and are happy.

When having fun and bringing joy to others is the focus of attention, negativity quickly fades away giving birth to a new dawn of happiness and Well Being.

Rascal is a very special dog who has earned a permanent place in our hearts. He has taught me a most valuable lesson in my mission of achieving unconditional love.

Rascal has clearly demonstrated the awesome power of focusing on having fun and bringing joy to others. When this is the focus of attention, negativity quickly fades away giving birth to a new dawn of happiness and Well Being. I often wonder, "Could Rascal be teaching me that bringing play and an element of fun to others is one of the ultimate expressions of unconditional love?"

DOG SECRETS as Whispered to the Dog Sitter

Do Nice Dogs Come In Last?

"Aggressive people are victorious!
Nice guys are losers!"

In the human animal world there is a saying, "Nice guys come in last." Most often I hear this saying when someone is referring to business matters where men engage in manipulative battles to achieve success. These business men's actions reflect the age-old belief that say, "If you are soft and meek you will be left behind; but, if you are aggressive/cut-throat you will rise to the top of the heap." This belief implies that, "Aggressive people are victorious! Nice guys are losers!"

Society has conditioned you to accept this belief. Right?

Both Herc and Skippy are nice guys. They are eight years old. Herc is a Bichon Poo, and Skippy is a Lapso-Apso Shih Tzu. They are neighborhood dogs and their owners brought them to my husband and me for dog sitting once every two weeks. The owners' believed that with time and familiarity we would bond with their dogs, and they would feel comfortable leaving them with us when they went away on vacations.

Because Herc and Skippy came on Thursdays they

would usually have the company of the young Golden Retriever named Carly, and the Chihuahua named Lacee. Both these dogs came for doggie daycare on Thursdays.

Realizing that dogs have their natural pecking order, I decided to let the natural way of the dogs prevail.

Because Carly and Lacee have been with us for over half a year, they informed me that they have first rights to our attention and to treats. They mutually agreed to make sure that Herc and Skippy knew who was boss and would take second place. In keeping with their agreement, Carly and Lacee uttered deep guttural sounds when Herc and Skippy attempted to move close to me while I was sitting on the couch. Also, when Herc raced to be first to receive his chicken jerky treat, both Lacee and Carly barked at him. Realizing that dogs have their natural pecking order, I decided to let the natural way of the dogs prevail. I figured that all was well as long as neither Herc nor Skippy were hurt.

Being older dogs (six years older than Lacee and Carly) and gentle dogs, Herc and Skippy would fade into the shadows of my consciousness. Although I knew they were present, they weren't demanding my attention like Carly and Lacee. Consequently, Herc and Skippy would spend much of their day resting on the couch lying next to each other. Snuggled-up together, they looked darling and content. Often I would pet them when I knew Carly and Lacee were not around to assert their one-upmanship.

After four visits, I began to yearn to know Skippy and Herc better. They were gentle, kind dogs—the type that are so pleasant and easy to have around as friends. It seemed that as I wished to know them better, my wish became a magnet that attracted some new behaviors. Carly and Lacee started accepting the rights of Herc and Skippy to be full pledged family members. They greeted Herc and Skippy with joy, sometimes even giving Herc and Skippy little licks. Responding to these kind gestures, Herc and Skippy played with their new friends and could often be seen snuggling up to their new canine friends. In regards to me, who was their dog sitting provider, Herc and Skippy became more outspoken. They told me what they wanted, and when they were pleased. For example, they would go to the door when they wanted to go out. Herc would follow me around the kitchen like my faithful companion waiting patiently until I would graciously present him with a "treat-from-heaven" falling his way. Herc's and Skippy's unique personalities were beginning to reveal themselves.

After three months of dog sitting, their owners, Julie and Chris, planned a week's vacation to Mexico. I looked forward to that week because I knew I would have time to get to know Herc and Skippy better.

To show their affection they would cuddle up tight against my leg.

When you have dogs, evenings become precious. Evenings are times when Raymond and I like to watch a little television or play cards and are more relaxed. This provided me with an opportunity to sit for a few hours on the couch. Skippy and Herc took advantage of the fact they were the only dogs present at night. Jumping up on the couch when they wanted some petting, they were never demanding. They were, however, very sweet. To show their affection they would cuddle up tight against my leg. Their soft and gentle touch of love became more and more precious, and I looked forward to this time alone with them. With gratitude, I petted them—my right hand petting Herc and my left hand petting Skippy. Dogs that once seemed so nice they faded into the shadows were emerging into the light. They were winning a place in my heart.

After relaxing for a while each night, it was bed time. Julie and Chris had told us, "Skippy and Herc like to sleep on the bed." Skippy was able to jump up onto our high bed, but Herc couldn't make the jump. After many attempts, Herc sadly resorted to his own little bed in the bedroom. Skippy settled himself in our bed after tenderly giving us good night licks/kisses.

Unfortunately during the night Skippy snuggled too closely next to Raymond preventing him from sleeping. I decided to take both dogs and go lay on the couch. With two dogs literally lying on top of me on our tiny couch, I was lucky to get any sleep myself. I told Raymond that I really wanted to pull out our sofa bed and sleep on it so both the dogs and I would be comfortable. Although Raymond didn't like sleeping apart from me, he understood that Skippy and Herc were used to human contact during the night. After some friendly persuasion, Raymond consented to my sleeping on our sofa bed with the dogs.

The next night I no sooner got under the covers when Herc and Skippy were at my side giving me good night dog kisses. This was their way of letting me know how much they appreciated my going to bed with them. During the night, Herc snuggled up next to me on my left side, and Skippy snuggled on my right side positioning himself up near my head. When I had to get up for my bathroom run, Skippy thoughtfully gave me permission to reposition him thereby enabling me to easily climb out of bed. In the morning, both dogs would wait until I was ready to get out of bed before making a racket.

As I write this story, Skippy and Herc are visiting with us. Their loving parents have gone skiing for the week end. This time when their parents let them off at our house for dog sitting, both dogs bounded in through the front door enthusiastically greeting us. While visiting with us, they had the company of one of their dear dog friends, whom they got to know during their last visit. His name is Riley, and he is a Bichon Poo. Riley is approximately six years old, and very sensitive (see the story called *Doggie in the Window.*)

I found that having nice dogs was a real treat, the worthiness of which continues to grow on me.

Being similar breeds, Riley and Herc not only looked alike, but were absolutely delighted to see each other again. It was fantastic to see these two rather shy dogs ecstatic to be in each other's company. Herc, Riley, Skippy and I went on a long walk for two hours with a neighborhood lady friend and her dog. It was fantastic to have the three dogs walk together with absolutely no quarrels and no snarls. Wow! What a relief! They didn't even bark when they passed new dogs on the path leading around the lake. What a joy! What a pleasure to have such nice, well behaved dogs. I found that having nice dogs was a real treat, the worthiness of which continues to grow on me.

Thinking about how Herc and Skippy were emotionally growing on me reminded me of my experience living in Costa Rica. When I was living there with the sun shining every day, month after month, it was so pleasant that the residents would say, "Living in Costa Rica is like living in Paradise, *Pura Vida.*" You see, when you live in Costa Rica, you don't have to worry about climate changes and other difficulties. As a result, you end up with more quality time spent in Real Nature—with the beautiful tropical flowers, the exquisite colorful birds and the howling monkeys. Okay, enough of that! Now onto my point!

Herc and Skippy are *so nice*, *so exquisite,* they are my *"Pura Vida".* The more I am with them, the more I reap the joyful awakening of their gentle, loving Natures. What magnificent dogs!

The worthiness of these two fur-balls as *nice dogs* propels them sky high ranking them as winners in my top echelon of Super Dogs.

Nice Dogs Are Winners!

Wow! Maybe we humans could learn something from the nice dogs.

All it requires is desire, good dog listening skills and unconditional love.

Do you think we are ready?

DOG SECRETS as Whispered to the Dog Sitter

Really?

***This story is told by Brody! The words are
Brody's words.***

My name is Brody. I am going to whisper my thoughts.
I'm doing this because I want to speak directly to you
through Blenda. You see, I truly like myself. I know
many of you don't like Pit Bulls because you fear the
breed. As a result of your fear, you don't like me. This is
my question: "Is this what you really want. Really?"

When I experienced dog sitting at Blenda and
Raymond's, it was quite an event. My owner, Pauline,
was talking to a friend trying to locate a dog sitter who
would take me. It seems many people are terrified
because I am an American Staffordshire terrier and in
the Pit Bull category. Although some people know that
the nature of Pit Bulls is gentle, most people are
brainwashed to believe Pit Bulls are dangerous. They are
brainwashed by stories—experiences of Pit Bulls who
are trained by their owners to be aggressive and cause
harm. Due to the brainwashing (myths), it is nearly
impossible to find anyone willing to dog sit a Pit Bull.
They don't want to take any chances of another dog in
their care being hurt. In my instance, it took Pauline's
friend to recommend accepting me.

I am going to share with you what happened during my

second dog sitting visit with Raymond and Blenda. Because their memories are a bit rusty, they vaguely remembered that on my first dog sitting visit a year prior they both ended up liking me. I became a bosom-buddy friend of Raymond's. He loved talking to me and hugging me. Blenda loved it when I sat on the couch next to her, and we watched television together. Perhaps it was time that dulled their memories, but I felt like Blenda and Raymond were suffering a bout of short-term amnesia.

This being the case, my faithful owner had to introduce me to them once again. I am eight years old, and I have been with Pauline a long time. There is no way she will ever abandon me. Anyway, Pauline put me in her truck, and a few minutes later we arrived at Raymond and Blenda's. They had a Chihuahua and a Miniature Dachshund that they were dog sitting. To test out whether I would be compatible, they asked my owner to take me into their large and fenced back yard. At first Pauline kept me on a leash. Of course I wanted to sniff the other dogs and play with them. I was annoyed when my owner constantly yanked my chain. Finally I got the message. Her message was, "I won't let you off this leash until you calm down. You are being tested. Be a good boy or this won't work."

I surrendered. I calmed down. Heck, I figured if I was good I would eventually be able to play with the dogs.

After a while, my owner let me loose. The little baby Dachshund named Rascal wanted to play. I started to chase him and all "you-know-what" broke loose. Blenda ran back and leaned against the house for safety, Raymond yelled at Rascal, and Pauline chewed me out in no uncertain terms. This was terribly hard for me, particularly when the little guy wanted to play with me. After all, we wanted to chase. Yeah, I'm twelve times bigger than Rascal, but so what? I am a very gentle dog. I know my strength and would do no harm.

After a while the three humans sat themselves down on lawn chairs. I guess they thought they would be safe sitting on the chairs. Anyway, they dared let me off-leash. I minded my p's and q's, at least most of the time. Very restless, the request that I remain subdued was torturing me. The Chihuahua named Lacee was actually an easy dog with whom I could deal. She had been with dogs like me and had no fear. Myself, I live with a Chihuahua so am used to having a good rapport with these little dogs. The Chihuahua wanted to play with the Dachshund, and that was driving me crazy because I wanted to have some fun with both dogs.

The Dachshund mostly hid under Blenda's chair. When I came over for a sniff, Blenda would get very nervous. After some heated discussion, she revealed the reason why she was nervous. She had been knocked over by a big dog and hurt. She didn't want a repeat. After what seemed like a long while, I sensed Blenda no longer wanted to be part of the testing. She went into the house. Fifteen more minutes later, everyone was convinced I would be okay for dog sitting.

There was, however, one more test. This time I met the Golden Retriever named Carly. We played outside under strict supervision. I could tell that Carly was not particularly fond of me, but would put up with me. When I tried to hump her, she refused and I was severely reprimanded.

Carly was in the kitchen lying by Blenda's feet. When they finally realized we were both in the house, they laughed.

Later, after I was accepted for dog sitting, Blenda and Raymond put me outside while Carly stayed inside. I felt like a second class citizen. I knew it was because they were afraid. This happens so often, it is a miracle I still like and approve of myself. Funny though, I did fool my dog sitters. I sneaked in and went to my bed in the living room where I laid down. Carly was in the kitchen lying by Blenda's feet. When they finally realized we were both in the house, they laughed. After that, Blenda and Raymond decided that as long as we were in separate rooms, we would be okay. This was a great victory for me because I did not enjoy rain beating down on me.

As I stayed with my new sitters, I earned their affection. Blenda opened her heart to me. Like on the first dog sitting visit, she invited me to lie next to her on the couch. I graciously accepted. This time it seemed to me like her petting had grown more tender and lasted longer.

As for Raymond, he had fun walking me as I am a fast walker and obedient. He also remembered what a Big Suck I am, and Raymond loves me that way. That is who I truly am, *One Big Suck*.

I write my story because maybe my story will help at least one person. I would like everyone to know that most of us Pit Bulls are just here to love and be loved. Yes, I understand you have been brainwashed to believe that all Pit Bulls are monsters to be feared. After hearing my story, I humbly ask you, "Do you really want to judge us Pit Bulls by the actions of a few—a few of us who have been bullied and trained to be aggressive? Really?"

Thank you for listening. Remember I love you!

Love and Licks from *One Big Suck*, Brody.

Naughty Dogs Are More Exciting

When something happens that is beyond co-incidence you know the Law of Attraction is working. I wondered why I would attract two dogs for dog sitting starting on the same day, coming from the same former doggie-daycare. Both dogs had matching caramel colored hair and their owners were middle aged working women. I couldn't help question, "What is the drawing factor that has attracted these two caramel colored puppies, one big and one small, into my life simultaneously?"

What I did know was that instantly my husband and I shared a home suddenly alive with puppy-like activity.

I didn't have the answers. What I did know was that my husband and I shared a home alive with puppy-like activity. Although of the same color, Carly, a Golden Retriever, is a big dog. In contrast, Lacee, a Chihuahua, is a small dog. Size wise, I figure it would take approximately four dogs Lacee's size to make one big dog Carly's size.

What made both dogs so interesting was that both were puppies. They loved to play. Carly was a mere four months old and Lacee over a year old, having come from Mexico as a rescue dog. According to her owner, named Jan, Lacee was one of approximately twenty Chihuahuas who were rescued in a group and shipped to Canada for adoption. Evidently Lacee was considered the most active and perhaps the most pesky of the whole group. So, even if she was a year older than Carly, Lacee was high strung, energetic and full of mischief.

I want to share with you an incident that demonstrates Lacee's high energy. Carly being rather unsuspecting would come up to Lacee and reach her paws out to her with a little dance that invited Lacee to play. In response, Lacee quickly raised her upper lip in a snarl accompanied by a deep growl saying in dog language, "Back off Carly. I am small but never doubt my power. I'm tough…a street dog born in Mexico! Grrr! You understand?"

For sure, Carly understood. Carly's backing off would be Lacee's cue that she had succeeded in showing Carly who was boss.

With her one-upmanship mission accomplished, Lacee would dart off in a rather teasing pompous manner. Not able to resist the tease, Carly would chase Lacee round the house. They ran from the living room into the kitchen, then into the hallway and back around into the living room in hot pursuit. After the tenth time, I would open the back door encouraging these canine mischief makers to continue their play outside.

If you come closer I will growl at you, and I know you can't tolerate my growl." In no uncertain terms Lacee reminds Carly that, "I am Leader of the Pack".

It is a riot to watch Carly and Lacee chase outside. Although Lacee is a small dog she can run so quickly that you can barely see her little feet as they fly through the air. Although Carly is right on Lacee's heels, she is always an inch behind Lacee. When Lacee finally gets winded she does one of her fast turnabouts and stands perfectly still. In dog language she says, "Come any closer to me, Carly, and I will growl at you. I know you can't stand it when I growl at you." In no uncertain terms Lacee reminds Carly that, "I am Leader of the Pack".

When Carly and Lacee finish chasing one another up and down the paths in the woods both dogs are worn out, happy, and a step closer to being best friends. Watching Carly tower over Lacee, Carly looks like she is the mother of Lacee. In reality, Carly is a very gentle and submissive dog and prefers Lacee being the Pack Leader.

When other dogs arrive at the house for dog-sitting, Carly and Lacee initiate them by putting them through the hoops. The only dog that has passed inspection a hundred percent is *sweet Casey* who comes five days a week. Casey is a real princess so I like to call her Princess Casey. Unfortunately Princess Casey went to Rainbow Bridge a couple months ago, but we who knew her will always remember Princess Casey fondly. She had a supernatural presence about her. When Lacee would snarl and snap at Princess Casey, Casey would respond by completely ignoring Lacee. Seeing that her attempts to scare Princess Casey had no impact, Lacee would back off and sometimes even return giving her a kiss saying, "I love and appreciate you." As for Carly, she would acknowledge Princess Casey with a nudge from her snout saying, "I think you are a cool elderly dog. I respect you."

A dog's behavior counseled me to realize, "Not being a member of the canine race, what I get to do is to respect the canine social and pecking order. I am the observer, not participant."

For the first half year when we were dog sitting these two dogs, Lacee would growl at newbies. Determined they would not invade her territory, she would continue snarling at these canine newbies until they acknowledged her house rules. The rules were simple: Lacee was pack leader and Top Dog Number One. This, of course, created a pecking order. Sometimes I would try to alter the pecking order. When I interceded, the best that would happen was that Lacee would calm down for a short while. Inevitably, the same pecking order would emerge. Finally I decided that dogs have their own dog language, their own pecking order, and they are going to do their own thing. A dog's behavior counseled me to realize, "Not being a member of the canine race, what I get to do is to respect the canine social and pecking order. I am the observer, not participant."

Learning to respect canine social structure is important. The longer I am with dogs, the more I leave them alone—both to play and settle their disputes. I have discovered that as I release my need for control, the faster the dogs calm down and become friends. In fact, as I am writing this story, Carly and Lacee are at our home with two other medium sized dogs. This is the first day all four dogs have been together. Remarkable! This time the initiation has only lasted five minutes and took place outside. As soon as all four dogs were safely settled inside the house, I ushered them outside where they proceeded to chase, bark and play. When they climbed back up the stairs and entered the kitchen through the back door, they were instant friends. Acknowledging their achievements and honoring the Dog-Hood of each of the dogs, I arranged their treats into four little piles. Individually, I handed each dog their treat. My purpose was to foster cooperation.

I have made progress overcoming my fears of dogs who do not know one another, particularly when they first meet and start fighting to establish who will be the dominant dog. To conquer my fears and create peace, I set an intention of unconditional love that will seed the atmosphere. Silly as this may sound, I was viewing a movie the other night called "People v the State of Illusion". It showed experiments where even inanimate objects were influenced by a nurturing atmosphere. In the experiment a metallic looking "random robot" was put in the center of a room, and it randomly wandered aimlessly around the entire room. Next chickens were put in the room and the robot was made to be still while the baby chickens gathered round the robot, often rubbing against it like they would a substitute mother. Next the chickens were fenced off in the right hand side of the room which was distant from the robot. This next time when the robot was set free to wander around the room, it only stayed in the right corner of the room where the chickens were. Although the Robot is an inanimate object, it had been influenced by the chickens—I suspect by their warmth and love.

I thought, "If an inanimate object can be influenced by little chickens, surely the dogs can be influenced by unconditional love.

I thought, "If an inanimate object can be influenced by little chickens, surely the dogs can be influenced by unconditional love. It makes sense that in an atmosphere of unconditional love, dogs are more relaxed. They will be able to accept new dogs as potential friends rather than as potential threats."

I believed that my efforts to extend unconditional love were paying off. Lacee and Carly's shortened initiation periods for the newbies were proof that seeding the atmosphere with unconditional love was working.

Dogs are my instructors. They teach me what I want to learn.

This thing about giving unconditional love was and continues to be a real challenge for me. I believe this is why I enjoy dog sitting so much. Dogs are my instructors. They teach me what I want to learn; in this case, how to better practice unconditional love. After all, don't we dog-lovers adore dogs because they are always there accepting us exactly the way we are? Heck! Just today I got an example of this. Raymond got upset because his computer was giving him a hard time. He sat down exhausted and cranky in his captain's chair. Sensing disturbance, Lacee moved over to me in my chair for comfort. I gave Lacee a big hug and held her until her body relaxed. Then I told Lacee, through my images that I sent to her mind, to please go over to Raymond in his Captain's chair and give him a little dose of love. Lacee got my message. She carefully walked over to Raymond and lay at his feet patiently waiting for him to invite her up.

Once in his arms, Lacee became the medicine Raymond needed. As for me, Lacee was teaching me the lesson that when I am willing to give, my own needs are answered. When I was co-creating with Lacee and giving Raymond the special love that he required, I found myself being pleasantly energized.

Unconditional love to me means giving love freely: without judgment, without fear, without trying to get something in return. It reminds me of the Hawaiian greeting "Aloha" that translated into English means, "The Divine Essence in me sees and greets the Divine Essence in you." To choose to practice unconditional love is one thing. To faithfully practice unconditional love is quite another matter, and often challenging as I was soon to discover.

This is what happened. Carly was by herself for dog-sitting. I had been cutting up some turkey, and she was in the kitchen watching my every move. I gave her some treats which encouraged Carly to remain glued to her begging spot. After I cut up the turkey, I prepared club sandwiches and soup for a special lunch. Seconds after pouring the soup, the phone rang. It was a business call, and I encouraged Raymond to take the call. As the sandwiches were ready, I put them on the dining room glass table and poured the soup back into the pot to stay hot. When Raymond finished the phone call, we went to the table. Guess what? Carly had eaten half my sandwich!

My gut instinct was to stick Carly's nose in the sandwich and tell her she was a **_Bad Dog_**! When I looked at Carly, however, she seemed totally innocent. Surmising Carly had finished her eating ten minutes ago and respectfully left me half the sandwich, I decided not to act based on my anger-driven instincts. Instead I lowered the plate to the level Carly could clearly see it, and then positioned her head so she was staring directly at the remainder of the sandwich. After I knew she had seen the sandwich, I went eyeball to eyeball with her and admonished, "No Carly. Next time leave the sandwich alone."

I know Carly heard me because afterwards she lay by my feet while I ate the other half. Strangely, I actually think Carly did me a favor because I would have stuffed myself eating that big sandwich. When Carly's owner came to pick her up, I related the sandwich incident. Cindy laughed and said Carly was trained not to eat off the kitchen counters; however, if goodies were left on a small to normal sized table, Carly treated that as fair game. Since our dining room table is glass and normal sized, it probably registered in Carly's brain as okay. Now it remains to be seen if Carly will remember that in our home the glass dining room table is out of bounds.

The jury is still out.

I wanted the dogs in my charge fully exercised to the point of being slightly worn out when their parents arrived for pick-up.

Another way these two playful puppies challenged me, and actually still challenge me, is on my daily walks. In the morning I typically take them both for a short walk on a leash. This is simple. If, however, I end up with more dogs than Lacee and Carly, Raymond comes to my rescue and walks Carly on his daily power walk. My big challenge comes with the afternoon walks. When I first started dog sitting, afternoons I would take the dogs for their second walk on-leash. Because the afternoon walk was longer, I believed I had done my duty providing the dogs with plenty of exercise. Then as I got more used to the dogs, I observed they were still filled with piss and vinegar at the end of the day. This was not what I wanted. I wanted the dogs in my charge fully exercised to the point of being slightly worn out when their parents arrived for pick-up. I figured this way the parents would know I had done a good job. If they wanted, they would have the option of relaxing rather than walking the dog after a hard day of work.

During the summer I had an epiphany. I was at the neighborhood lake with Princess Casey who is the Pomeranian dog I could let off-leash. Because I completely trusted Princess Casey, I could go for my own swim in the lake. This particular afternoon while swimming, I saw a dog also swimming in the lake for a ball. The dog was a Golden Retriever and reminded me of Carly. When I got out of the water, the Golden Retriever was called Carly by an elderly couple. I wondered, "Could this be our Carly?" Sure enough, it was. Carly was out with Cindy's neighbors, off-leash. She was running loose retrieving the ball from the water.

"Well," I thought to myself, "if the neighbors can let Carly run loose, so can I."

The next day when Carly arrived for dog-sitting, I decided to take the big plunge. I put Carly and Lacee in the car and drove down to the path leading to the lake. My heart was beating twenty miles an hour. Yes, I was scared! I opened the car door, put Lacee on a leash and let Carly run free. Carly didn't waste a second. She took off like greased lightning making a beeline down the long curving path towards the lake. I watched as Carly disappeared into the distance. Out of necessity, I released control; there was no way Carly could hear me when I tried calling her. Besides, even if Carly could hear me, it would be a stroke of luck if she complied with any request.

All Carly had on her mind was the lake. Tugging Lacee on her leash, I raced after Carly. When I finally reached the beach Carly was standing at the edge of the lake. She was waiting for me. Carly wanted me to throw the ball into the water so she could retrieve it. If only Carly knew how relieved I was that she was standing there safe.

She acted like I had just given her the best present in the whole wide world. Her tail was wagging above the water as she swam back to shore with ball in her mouth.

Happily I threw the ball. Carly swam quickly and regally to retrieve the ball. She acted like I had just given her the best present in the whole wide world. Her tail was wagging above the water as she swam back to shore with the ball in her mouth. Once on shore, Carly shook herself spraying water all over me. Then Carly dropped her ball and patiently waited for me to pick it up so I could throw it again. I congratulated myself, "Wow! This is actually working. My risk-taking is worthwhile. Carly is off-leash and all is well. All dogs and humans are safe!"

Having succeeded thus far, I decided to take the other half of the plunge. I decided to let our little frisky

Chihuahua, Lacee, off-leash. This was a huge risk because Lacee has a nasty habit of barking aggressively at every dog she encounters. This particular habit makes me queasy. I was not sure if Lacee would attack another dog or person. Needing encouragement, I spoke to myself and said, "Gosh darn it! Lacee deserves an opportunity to be off-leash and run freely. I have to dare myself and take the risk."

I counted: "One, two three…GO!"

I bent down and held my breath, as if believing that holding my breath would grace me with good luck. With Lady Luck on my side, I set Lacee free. Off-leash, Lacee darted from tree to tree. Then seeing another dog approaching the swimming area, true to form, Lacee started barking at the dog. In this case, the dog she was barking at was a big Black Lab. Again, I held my breath hoping that things would work out. Realizing hope was not enough, I forced myself to inhale deep breaths of air literally jump-starting myself to move into a relaxed, confident state of KNOWING all was in "Divine Right Order."

Lacee continued to bark at the Black Lab, but did not nip or bite the dog. Thank goodness!

The Black Lab turned and started going his own way. Oops! Then, as if to have the final say the way women often do, Lacee decided to follow the Lab barking aggressively at him. This got the Black Lab's attention. The Lab started running around and next thing I knew both dogs were having a ball chasing each other.

"Wow!" I was surprised. Ready to celebrate this victory, I told myself, "Now I deserve a big sigh of relief. The dogs are safe. I am safe. The dogs are happy. I am in Seventh Heaven."

I patted myself on the back congratulating myself, "Indeed, I took a big risk letting the dogs run free. I trusted I could project calm reassurance (or at least a semblance of calmness). And, I did it! I succeeded and the proof is in the pudding!"

While writing about this, I am thinking that many people may think that letting dogs off-leash is no big thing. I know when Raymond and I owned our own dogs, I would let them off leash. Recalling our experiences, I realize it wasn't a big deal because I started training the dogs when they were puppies. When you are an ordinary person (not a dog trainer) and you are dog-sitting, letting a dog off-leash is not the same as letting your own dog off-leash. Suddenly you find yourself keenly aware that if anything happens to one of the owner's precious dogs, you will be held accountable. Like with Lacee, already Jan had told me that many times Lacee has run away from her and she has spent many anxiety-ridden hours tracking Lacee down. Listening to Jan, logically I think, "If Lacee runs away from her Mom, what is going to stop her from running away if I let her off-leash. If I could not find Lacee, what the heck would I ever tell her Mom. I can't even imagine what I would do…it is too frightening to comprehend."

"I can do this! All I have to do is believe and remember that what I believe I will achieve."

Then to muster up my courage I would think, "Gosh! I can do this! All I have to do is believe and remember that what I believe I will achieve. Therefore, I logically reasoned, "I believe that Lacee knows that she must behave with me, that I am too old to go running after her, and that it is to her benefit to listen to me and come when I call her." Choosing to focus on these beliefs, I brain-washed myself into believing I was the Pack-leader and could assume a state of calm command. Armed with these beliefs as my "rod and staff" comforting me, I would build up my confidence by frequently beckoning Lacee back to my side. When Lacee complied, and she did, I patted her on the head reassuring her. This was her reward—not food, but a demonstration of my affection. I was proud of Lacee and happy with our off-leash walking accomplishments.

Now, as for Carly, I didn't have to worry about her being aggressive. She was an Angel Ambassador. She would joyfully befriend all the dogs she met. The only time Carly got into trouble was when I was returning to the car. Carly would race ahead of me and when she reached the car would gallivant onto the street. This scared the heck out of me because one never knows what kind of driver is coming around the bend. Fortunately, after yelling several times at Carly, she heard me and came. Like many dog parents when your dog has done something wrong that threatens their safety, you are so darn happy to see them that any scolding you had planned takes second place. This was the case with Carly.

WOW! Having successfully overcome my fear of letting the dogs loose at the lake, guess what? There was an even bigger challenge awaiting me. You see, I knew it wouldn't be too difficult to let Carly and Lacee free at the lake because there was only one single path to run down and it ended at the lake. There was little chance either dog would run into the bushes because there weren't many. So, while the swim hole at the lake was great, it wasn't where I wanted to take the dogs every day. I really preferred to take them to a place where they could reap the rewards of a good long run.

As if to answer my request, the power greater than myself led me up Skyline Drive, way up the hill. Then with a left turn at the top of the long windy hill, I was led to the end of that road. Here there was a gate decked out in yellow paint. I parked my car determined to explore this new hidden opportunity. The wide path wandered through a tranquil forest setting. When I took the right fork in the path it meandered lead me down to a deserted old clearing that once was a park. It was about a fifteen minute walk to the secluded quaint park. Instantly I knew this was the exact right place to take the dogs. I could let them loose, off-leash that is, if I could muster up the courage.

Fortunately for me, at this time the little Pomeranian dog was still alive. Princess Casey was an excellent walker off-leash and would faithfully come to me when I called her. In my mind's eye I could picture her helping me train the other two dogs. With Casey as Dog Instructor, I decided to put my plan into action. My plan was to first train Lacee, and second to train Carly.

Adding vivid mental pictures to my request was fun. When I called Lacee and in imagination pulled her back to me via the rope, she raced back to me.

I piled all three dogs into our van and drove up Skyline Drive to my new secret hide-away. First out the car door was Princess Casey. Next I put Carly on her leash and let her out of the car. When it looked like the coast-was-clear, I released Lacee from her leash. She was totally free. Lacee was so excited. She dashed all around like a little school girl loose on the playground. At the entrance of the path stood two older style farm houses, and Lacee raced toward one of the houses to investigate it. Immediately I got to try out my Pack Leader skills. I called, "Come back Lacee. Come back now!" She ignored me. I told myself to stay calm. I called Lacee a second time with as much calm authority as I could muster up. This time Lacee responded to my command. Walking up the little hill along the path, I made sure that Lacee was in my line of sight. If she strayed too far, I would summon her to me. I used my imagination picturing there was a long invisible rope stretching between us. Adding vivid imaginary pictures was fun. In imagination, when I called Lacee, she came back right away. In reality, nine out of ten times Lacee responded immediately.

Yes, true there were some instances when Lacee simply went her own way. This is when Princess Casey came to the rescue. She was like a herd dog. She would go and engage Lacee in playing, and as part of the play would coax her into view. Princess Casey was so attuned to me and my inner wishes that her presence was like that of a guardian angel—dog style, of course. She is a marvelous dog. My heart tells me that as I am writing this Princess Casey is watching over me from Rainbow Bridge in doggy Heaven.

When I look back at the situation, I think either I was a bit nuts to let Lacee go off-leash first, or I had such a strong faith that it empowered my positive visualizations.

Needless to say, I was most happy with the success we were having. If you can picture me, you will appreciate my precarious situation. Intent on keeping track of

Lacee, I also had Carly on-leash constantly tugging. Carly was letting me know in no uncertain terms that she wanted to be free like the other two dogs. When I look back at the situation, I think either I was a bit nuts to let Lacee go off-leash first, or I had such a strong faith that it empowered my positive visualizations. In truth, it was probably a bit of both: being a bit nuts combined with strong faith.

With Lacee learning to walk off-leash, we went to our secret walking spot about three times a week—always with our guardian angel, Princess Casey. Each time my confidence grew. Finally I was relaxed even when Lacee was not in sight. With patience and perseverance, Lacee was proving to be a great dog. She returned to me when I called her.

Two weeks passed, and at an intuitive level I knew Lacee's training was complete. I knew this because while I walked I would occasionally daydream. When I returned to normal conscious awareness, nothing had changed. Both dogs and I were safe and well.

Once Lacee's training was complete, it was time to think about letting Carly off-leash. Now I had the opportunity to enlist both Princess Casey and Lacee as my herd dogs. Even though I would have both dogs helping me when I tried imagining Carly off-leash, I discovered I was fearful. I had two fears. The first fear was that Carly would get so rambunctious in her play that she would knock me over, possibly injuring me. The second fear is that Carly might decide to take off exploring. If Carly ran off, there was zero chance I could catch up to her. To overcome these fears, I decided that I would ask my friend, Steven, to do the walk with me. I knew Steven was good with dogs and had that masculine commanding voice that works so well in dog obedience.

Steven agreed, and we began our walk. He let Carly loose and guess what? Carly immediately came back when Steven called her. When Carly returned to Steven she could easily have knocked him over. I don't know how he did it, but Steven had a miraculous way of getting Carly to come to a grinding halt right before his feet.

As we walked further, Carly sniffed the bushes, explored, and had fun bugging Lacee. Carly loved to bug Lacee until Lacee dashed off with Carly hot in pursuit after her. They ran round in circles so fast I was thankful Steven was present. This way I could hide behind him in self-defense—just so the dogs wouldn't accidently knock me down.

After Steven's help, I knew the dress rehearsal was over. It was my time to brave letting Carly off-leash—all by myself. Armed with cell phone, whistle and plenty of prayer, I believed I was ready. I climbed out of our car and put Carly on her leash. When we got to the path I made sure there were no other dogs in sight, and then prayed that I would be able to complete this feat. When I bent down to let Carly off-leash, I was light headed. The only way I could get myself to let her loose was to pray...pray we were safe and protected. With this prayer, I let Carly loose. She galloped down the path like a horse just let out to pasture. She was a pure delight to watch. Carly is so smart, I believe she intuitively heard my prayer. Heck, in reality, I had no cause to worry as Princess Casey and Lacee were on stand-by. They were ready to activate their herding duties. Princess Casey and Lacee knew the sacred path like their own back yard.

Both dogs raced past me missing me by mere inches.

After running free for fifteen minutes, Carly decided to play. She started chasing Lacee. This time I decided to stand my ground and not duck or run away. Both dogs raced past me missing me by mere inches. My heart jumped as it brought back memories of my being knocked down by a big dog in the dark behind our former Virginia Beach home. Although I didn't break any bones, I was on pain medication for a month. I'm sure it is this past experience that has made me fearful of being knocked down by some overzealous dog.

Well, the walk was a total success. We did make it back to the car safely. I was relieved it was over and all went well. Now Carly and Lacee can burn off excess energy with a well-earned good run. This probably would not be possible if other people frequented this secret hideaway; therefore, I have only told one other dog owner where it is located.

As Lacee is a barker, I prefer not to meet other dogs when Lacee is with me. One time I was walking Lacee and Tink, who is a Pug dog, on our secret path. When we were almost back at the car, I became a bit careless. Another lady with two dogs on-leash was approaching me. I was going to bend down and put Lacee on-leash but the lady yelled, "Don't worry. It will be okay."

Lacee raced up to the lady barking ferociously at her and nearly nipping her ankles. In response, the lady became frightened and physically held onto one of her dogs so it wouldn't lunge at Lacee. I saw the owner was having a rough time. I yelled at Lacee to come back. It took a long time for Lacee to respond. By the time she returned to my side, I was extremely upset and nervous. As I went to put Lacee back on-leash, I accidently let go of the Pug's leash. He took off after the lady. Fortunately the lady was able to shoo Tink away, and reluctantly he returned to me.

Biting my tongue, I decided the best response was no response.

Wow! Was I grateful everyone was safe. The lady who had been so nice couldn't resist admonishing me, "You should have your dogs on a leash. If your dogs were on a leash this wouldn't have happened." Biting my tongue, I decided the best response was no response. Thankful and yet shaken up, I returned to the car and didn't tell anyone about the incident lest I get negative feedback. I didn't want this experience to change my mind and convince me to decide to abandon my "off-leash" walks.

Little did I know that Princess Casey was soon going to pass away. Now that she is in doggie Heaven at Rainbow Bridge, it is just Lacee and Carly. Although we miss Princess Casey, we bless her and her pioneer "off-leash" instruction. I know Carly really misses Princess

Casey because on her last day, while she was lying on the couch, several times Carly went up to her and kissed her right on the cheek.

Lacee and Carly are still naughty dogs, but this really doesn't matter. In actual fact, it gives me a pleasant challenge. My current project is to do my best to train Lacee, who is temperamental by virtue of being a Chihuahua, to stop barking when on leash. She barks whenever she sees another dog. As my solution, when we spot another dog I'm relaxing my grip on her leash so Lacee experiences a calm, confident feeling of me being in control; or, sometimes I make a ninety degree turn and start walking the other direction so the disruptive dog is no longer in sight. These tips to stop a dog from barking are Cesar Milan's. I'm sure they work, but I still have a long ways to go before I master them. That's why naughty dogs are great. They keep me alert, active and on my toes!

I can't wait to see what new adventures await me!

The Sweetest Dog in the Whole Wide World

Have you ever caught yourself saying to your dog, "You are the best dog in the whole wide world?" I have told this to every dog I have owned. When I started dog sitting I discovered I could no longer say this since I had several dogs for whom I was caring. Although every dog seemed to merit a place of being the best dog, I knew that if I rated one dog as being best, I would automatically be judging the other dogs as less than perfect.

With Casey I admit that often I indulged in believing she was the best dog in the whole wide world. Still, I couldn't bring myself to reserve this "best dog" spot for one dog when I loved each of the dogs in my care. Consequently, I was delighted when one day it dawned on me that Casey was the sweetest of all the doggies I dog-sat. With this new insight, I could honestly say to Casey, "Casey, you are the *sweetest dog* in the whole wide world."

Casey is not only the *sweetest dog* in the whole wide world, but also a very special dog with a very special story. I am honored to be able to tell you about Casey and share her story that she whispered to me.

How Casey came to Raymond and me for dog sitting is a

story in itself. The downstairs suite in our four-plex home was for rent. It seemed that no one wanted to move in and so it sat empty for nearly two months. Then one evening I was returning from walking the dogs, it was dark out, and there was a lady walking away from the door next to ours—the door where the Property Manager resides. I briefly introduced myself to the lady who told me her name was Gabriela and that she had just rented the suite below us. So that Gabriela would be pre-warned I said, "Oh! It is a pleasure to meet you. My husband and I will be your neighbors. We live upstairs and are dog sitters."

Gabriela turned to her friend who was accompanying her and said, "How fantastic! I get two blessings in one evening—a new home and a dog sitter. I have a dog and will need dog sitting. I work five days a week." Approximately one week later Gabriela moved into her suite, and I had an opportunity to meet her eight year old Pomeranian female dog named Casey.

I have to admit, my first impression of Casey was clouded with judgment. Although Casey was very friendly, I thought she was rather pudgy. Much as I tried to ignore her pudginess and not judge her because of it, for some weird reason, in this case I was not able to extricate myself from my judgments.

Realizing I would be better off overcoming my prejudice, to help me I decided to use an old memory of something that happened to me and made a big difference in my life. Being a relationship therapist, I knew that men usually judge women by the beauty of their physical bodies, while women usually judge men by their personality that shines forth displaying their *True Character*. Keeping this in mind, I focused in on an experience I had while attending a conference.

When Mark was introduced, I thought he was ugly as sin with a beard and being unshaven. Although he was ugly, Mark was a charismatic speaker and delivered an impassioned talk with joy and eloquence. I leaned forward listening intently to every word Mark had to say. I became so engrossed in the talk and who Mark was that my whole perception changed. By the end of his thirty minute speech, my perception of Mark totally transformed—I honestly saw him as being a very handsome man.

> ***"If I focus my attention on a quality of Casey I like, that is her friendly nature, I will transform my perception and see Casey as a sweet dog who is highly feminine and pretty.***

Using the memory of this experience, I told myself, "If I focus my attention on a quality of Casey I like, that is her friendly nature, I will be able to transform my perception and see Casey as a *sweet dog* who is highly feminine and pretty. Because 'Thoughts become things' my thoughts will create new experiences." In this case, my new perceptions were creating some wonderful new experiences for me. Now when I looked at Casey, what I saw was a sweet, adorable puppy dog.

Right from the get-go when I started dog sitting Casey, I was happy to have her around. She was easygoing and frequently shook her fanny and wagged her tail exuding her feminine, friendly nature.

As I got to know Casey better three quirks stood out.

Number One Quirk:

When Casey came through the back door in the morning she would immediately sniff around the kitchen looking for any goodies from Heaven that might have dropped to the floor. After completing her sniffing rounds, Casey would beg for her treat telling me, "I have arrived. I am your gift, your treasure, and I deserve to be rewarded."

Number Two Quirk:

Casey would love to be near me while I was sitting at the computer. I am at the computer a lot and Casey would patiently lay by my feet hour after hour. I have to tell you, having a dog lay at your feet is "real gold". Casey's patient loving energy created a soft stream of loving energy flowing from my feet up to my heart and then up to my noggin-brain for some greatly appreciated noggin massaging. When you are a writer, this is a dream come true.

Number Three Quirk:

Casey delighted me with a little dance she performed when I leaned down to put on my walking shoes. This was her signal that it was time for a W-A-L-K. She would dance round in little circles and end by rubbing her fanny against the carpet. Evidently she got so excited it made her fanny itch. When I climbed down the stairs to the front door, Casey would be right by my side sticking to me like glue. She wanted to make sure she wouldn't accidently be left behind.

Actually, I just lied. In Truth, there is one more of Casey's quirks that really stood out. Now that I have your curiosity, I will keep you in suspense until later in the story.

As I began to look forward to Casey's daily quirks, I changed and my original prejudice completely disappeared. Every day Casey and I grew closer together. Not only was Casey bonding with me and my husband, but we were bonding with her. After a couple of months of dog-sitting Casey, I eagerly looked forward to her scratching at our back door announcing she was ready to be our dog for the day.

Intuition is so much fun and is a great tool. How I used it with Casey was to become still, center myself in peace, listen to what Casey was saying to me through actions and energy and then use my intuition to respond.

Although Casey was already trained, there was always more to do. I can't say I am the world's best trainer as I have never had lessons. What I do possess and what has worked for me (and I think Caesar Milan approves of) is Intuition. Intuition is so much fun and is a great tool. How I used it with Casey was to become still, center myself in peace, listen to what Casey was saying to me through actions and energy and then use my intuition to respond. For instance, if I sensed that Casey was bored or feeling like she needed an emotional boost, I would pick her up and give her lots of hugs and whispers of "love n' sweet nothings."

I trusted *Thought Pictures for Training.*

As I believe I mentioned previously, for seventeen years I enjoyed my own private counseling practice. As part of my sessions, often I would describe to my client how dogs respond to our "Thought Pictures". Here is my example: Imagine you are on the couch and your dog named Thor is sitting opposite you on a chair. You want Thor to come to you. If you think, "Thor, I don't want you on the chair," then Thor will visualize himself on the chair, that you want him to stay on the chair, and will not come to you. Instead if you think, "Thor, I want you to jump down off the chair and walk over to me at the couch and lay by my feet," then Thor will have received a clear picture of what you want—just like in a movie! Thor will get off the chair, walk over to where you are sitting on the couch, and lay at your feet.

Providing your energy is loving and commanding, the process of using pictures to communicate is very effective. First your dog will respond to your energy, and then to your "Thought Pictures.'' When both are in synch, your wish is your dog's command.

I believe one hundred percent in "Thought Pictures" for training. I have fond memories of training my former dog named Chipper regarding his walking with me. I accomplished this by visualizing Chipper walking by my side. Using this technique, when I would stop at the curb and wait before crossing the busy street, my dog would also stop. Although Casey was not my own, it became second nature for me to train her. Using "Thought

Pictures," I trained Casey to walk by my side and not run away. This came in very handy when walking along paths and in the forest at Goldstream Park. Casey was so attuned to my energy and my "Thought Pictures" that I could let her loose with no leash. Meanwhile, for safety purposes, most of the other dogs would be on-leash.

Since Casey refused to be a target for their bullying, the other dogs would give up.

Casey was a fast learner. It didn't take her long to realize that she was special and treated with distinguished honor. In response to the special place of honor awarded her, Casey became my helper and a teacher. She would befriend the other dogs that came for dog sitting by helping them relax and feel safe in our loving home. For example when one of the dogs would bark at Casey, trying to rile her, she would confidently stand-her-ground. Because Casey wouldn't budge, the attempt of the other dog to "get her goat" would fail. Since Casey refused to be a target for their bullying, the other dogs would give up. After the bullying attempt was over, usually I would spot the other dog talking to Casey and "yes," sometimes even giving Casey a lick on the face. Amazingly, this happened with small dogs as well as with large dogs including with Boxers and Pit Bulls.

Finally, Number Four Quirk:

What really stood out was her fearless ability to stand her ground with any dog. With this amazing ability, Casey could make friends with any person or dog and never be bullied. She had absolutely no fear and earned a reputation of being a real *SWEET DOG!* As Casey made friends with new dogs, they relaxed and felt comfortable in their "home away from home".

> *Casey's ego was intact and she didn't need to be Pack Leader. Her life didn't revolve around having power and dominance.*

Funny thing, although Casey received special privileges she still longed to be treated like an ordinary dog. When we went dog walking there were many instances when two dogs would walk together on my leash-made-for-two, and Casey would not be on a leash. While walking, Casey would position herself between the two dogs and then start walking with them. If looking from a distance, you would think all three dogs were walking together on a three pronged leash. Hard as I tried to read Casey's mind, I was never sure exactly what she was thinking. What I like to think is that Casey was simply telling the other dogs that even though she was being treated special, with her dog friends she preferred to be considered an ordinary dog like them. She wanted to be their friend with no strings attached. Casey's ego was intact and she didn't need to be Pack Leader. Her life didn't revolve around having power and dominance.

This may seem nutty, but while walking I love to sing to the dogs. I like singing to the dogs because it doesn't matter if I sing off key, and I imagine that the dogs appreciate my kind words. Picking up my joy, the dogs wag their tails in delight. With Casey I was lucky because one of her best friends who often walked with her was a little Chihuahua named Lacee. That made it easy for me to rhyme my songs by using the names Lacee and Casey. I would sing, "Casey and Lacee are good dogs, are good dogs, are good dogs. Casey and Lacey are good dogs and I love them so." Well, okay, the words are repetitive and certainly not fancy, but they were filled with joy. As the dogs listened to my silly singing, they would wag their tails and trot lightly on their feet to the beat of my notes.

Over the months Casey bonded more closely with my husband and me. We felt like we were Casey's second home—her second set of parents and her "home away from home". When Gabriela's son, named Ben, came to live with Gabriela for four months, we only got Casey about once a week because Ben was home and willing to walk her. This was great for Casey and I have to admit that during this long stretch of time often I was lonely for Casey's company. How I would satisfy myself was to look out the living room window where frequently I would see Ben walking Casey on her leash up to Goldstream Park. Ben would take Casey on a longer and more rigorous walk than I did, and this absolutely thrilled Casey.

To accomplish this personal challenge of demonstrating unconditional love, I learned to replace my loneliness with empathy and gratitude.

Looking out the window I would see Casey's entire body quivering with delight. I would remember that unconditional love meant being grateful for the other party (whether human or canine) when they were happy.

To accomplish this personal challenge of demonstrating unconditional love, I learned to replace my loneliness with empathy and gratitude. I was thankful Casey was getting these long, exciting and healthy walks with Ben. I consciously made the decision to change my thoughts from loneliness to gratitude. As I accomplished this, I felt emotionally fulfilled. Casey and Ben were great teachers and *Sweet Casey* deserved our love.

Now, this could be my imagination, but to me this was a real experience. There were a few times when neither Ben nor Gabriela were at home, thus leaving Casey alone in their downstairs suite. Although I could not hear Casey, I sensed her pain at being left alone. My Intuition spoke so loudly to me that sometimes it felt like it was shouting at me. My Soft Self wanted to race downstairs, give Casey a hug, and bring her upstairs. My Rational Self knew this solution did not respect the intimate bonding of Casey to Gabriela and Ben. So, what I chose to do was to quiet myself and tell my Intuition to whisper in Casey's ear that I loved her very much and she was not alone. Then I would create a picture in my mind that I was emotionally putting my arms around Casey and embracing her. Of course, I expected Casey to be picking up my clear image. Having done this, I fully believed that Casey was feeling better. For certain, I felt better!

After four months, Ben departed to take a new job. His new job involved being trained as a professional chef and required his going to Germany. We would all miss him, and this includes Casey. You see, Ben had chosen

Casey to be his Mom's dog. Casey had been running loose and looking for a home. Ben made arrangements for Casey to come live with his Mom. This was very powerful because Casey already loved Gabriela. Gabriela lived alone and frequently Casey had come scratching at her door for a visit. So, when Ben departed for Germany there was an empty place in all our hearts.

When Ben left, Casey again stayed with us five days a week while her Mom worked. When Casey returned, I did my best to give her some extra-long walks at Goldstream Park—I wanted her to know I was doing my very best to make up for her loss of Ben's great walks and to insure her happiness. Casey seemed to understand. In the morning she would bound up the steps to the back door, scratch the door, and again let me know she was ready to be our dog for the day. What a darling, furry little gift of love. I wanted to show my appreciation, so after Casey had come in and received her little treat, I would go into the living room to the couch where Casey would join me for special hugs. Together we would spend glorious days, and again Casey would greet the new dogs making sure they were comfortable in their new "home away from home". At night when her Mom returned from work, Casey greeted her with licks and love. Casey is remarkable. She has enough love to encircle the globe many times over. What a dog! What a Dog Spirit Light-Being!

Dogs are Metamorphytes and that means that they mold themselves to their owners taking on their personality traits.

131

Of course, I have to give Gabriela credit. Dogs are Metamorphytes (I think maybe my husband invented this word) and it means that they mold themselves to their owners taking on their personality traits. Perhaps this is why Casey was so loving and sweet. Gabriela practiced unconditional love. There are many examples of Gabriela's unconditional love, and one that I remember and cherish involves Casey at the beach. When Casey would be walking on the beach with Gabriela and spot a friendly family, she would run up to them with tail a-wagging and then rub up against them greeting them with her *Sweet Hellos*. The lucky people would smile and start petting Casey. Casey warmed their hearts. This never could have happened if Gabriela had punished Casey for her extreme friendly behavior. Instead Gabriella would smile and say, "That's my Casey girl. She loves everybody!"

Before I forget, I want to add another accomplishment onto Casey's list. After Casey learned to respond affirmatively to my training her off-leash by "Thought Picture" commands, she let me know she would be willing to assist me in off-leash training of her Chihuahua friend, Lacee. I believed this would be quite a "fait accompli" as Lacee's Mom told me that when she lets Lacee off-leash she often runs away. Sometimes she has spent many hours tracking Lacee down. Being in charge of dog sitting, I could not allow this to happen. I took Casey and Lacee to a secret walking place I had discovered near our home. Here there is a large path that wanders into a small deserted park in the woods. Wrapping myself in Love's protection, I let Lacee off-leash. She darted here and there among the trees. When Lacee wandered off course, Casey would corral her. With a mixture of joy and relief, I would see both dogs reappear. Together they walked, ran and played. Rarely have I ever seen Casey and Lacee so happy. This became a wonderful outing for them and proved very good for both dogs to run off steam. I was glad I took the risk and had faith in Casey helping me.

Overall, Casey was a satisfied, happy dog. Five days a week she visited with Raymond and me, and for four of those days there were friends with whom she could play. When her friends went home around dinner time, Casey often shared a couple of additional hours with us as her Mom worked late. Then when her Mom arrived home, Casey gladly accompanied her Mom to share their very special bond of love. As part of their special sharing, every other week-end Casey would enjoy a long car ride with her Mom.

All relationships involving Casey were marvelous. Then one day around December 14^{th,} Casey came to the back door, walked in and sniffed the kitchen but did not beg for her Chicken Jerky Tender treat. I thought to myself, "This is strange. Oh well, her Mom said that Casey hadn't eaten her breakfast and not to worry, so I guess

Casey simply isn't hungry." I put the piece of Chicken Jerky Tender down near where Casey slept at my feet believing eventually she would eat it." I picked Casey up and carried her into the living room where we enjoyed our usual hugs on the couch. About half an hour later the Golden Retriever, Carly, arrived for dog-sitting. Carly wanted to play with Casey, but Casey wasn't in the mood. Casey positioned herself under the dining room table where she would not be disturbed. Alarmed, I brought Casey her breakfast. This was the first time in eight months that she did not touch her dog food. I was worried.

I decided to call Gabriela. I looked for Casey's intake papers where Gabriela's work number would be listed. Evidently we had never bothered to update Casey's papers and so her work number was not listed. Luckily I found Gabriela's cell number and called her. I could not get through. It sounded like Gabriela had suspended her cell service. I knew Gabriela worked at a hotel, but did not know the name of it. My heart started to pound. I walked down into Gabriela's suite thinking there might be an envelope or piece of paper with the hotel name on it. There was nothing in sight and I didn't feel right searching her drawers. A shiver of unwanted fear ran down my spine! Darn! Now I had no way to get hold of Gabriela by phone.

Running out of options, I wrote Gabriela an email in case she looked at her emails while at work. Then I prayed. I prayed that Casey would get better. I sent Casey all the love I knew how to send. Gently I lifted her up on the couch and wrapped her like a baby in my bathrobe. I wanted Casey to smell my scent and know I loved her every moment. Instinctively I knew she was in pain. I left Casey alone to sleep, thinking that sleep would be good for her healing. I sensed she was losing energy quickly, and she seemed to hurt when she exerted herself. Her pain and sudden loss of energy was happening so quickly I was worried.

Hours passed. Afternoon arrived. I took Carly for her walk leaving Casey on the couch for healing purposes. When I returned, Casey was standing at the top of the staircase looking sadly at me. She wanted to know why I had not taken her for a walk. I lifted Casey up into my arms and carried her down the stairs to see if she wanted to go on her own special walk. Slowly and gently we walked a couple of blocks. Then I turned around and headed home. I was frightened and did not want to overdo it. Although I considered calling the Vet, I did not call because I believed it was not my right to contact the vet without Gabriela's consent.

Night arrived. It was a very tough night. Gabriela had her company party and was scheduled to come home late. She had told me not to wait up for her. She recommended I put Casey downstairs and that Casey would be okay by herself for a couple of hours before she returned. Raymond asked me if I was going to put Casey downstairs as it was almost 10:00 pm and our bed time. I replied, "There is no way I am going to leave Casey alone."

When I touched Casey's tummy, she whimpered. I knew

she was hurting, and did not know what was wrong. I changed into my bathrobe, and decided I would sleep on the couch with Casey until her Mom arrived. I was ready to turn off the lights when I heard Gabriela's car pull into the driveway. I went outside and told Gabriela that Casey was upstairs with me. I asked her to please join us when she was ready.

> *Gabriela went to Casey and as she gently stroked Casey's body, you could see the love and concern flowing from her hands and heart to Casey.*

Gabriela knocked on the back door. I let her in. Wow! Did she look great in her beautiful black cocktail dress. Here she was so happy, and I had dreadful news to impart. I can never describe to you how awful it felt to tell my good friend and neighbor that her precious dog was very sick and laying on the couch in the other room. There are no words to adequately capture this heart-wrenching task.

Gabriela went over to where Casey was lying. As she gently stroked Casey's body, you could see the love and concern flowing from her hands and heart to Casey. Like me, Gabriela had no idea what was the matter. Concerned, she lifted Casey into her arms. Carefully she walked over to the back door and in her elegant high heels descended down the steep fifteen back stairs. Holding back tears, I watched as Gabriela disappeared into the shadows and into her own suite. I couldn't help but wonder if this might be the last time I would see Casey. I had to fight back running to Casey and telling her one more time how much I loved her.

Shortly after Casey left, it hit me like a ton of bricks. Instantly, I knew what was wrong with Casey. She must have some obstruction in her tummy that rapidly got worse during the day. The answer seemed clear as day. I realized that this was one time when fear had blocked my Intuition. "Interesting," I thought, "shortly after Casey was safely turned over to Gabriela, the answer was revealed to me."

Fortunately Gabriela had the next day off. She took Casey to her Vet. The Veterinarian clinic x-rayed her and discovered Casey had something stuck in her tummy. The x-ray technicians had no idea what it was except that it was rectangular in shape. The clinic said they could operate to remove it but weren't sure if they would be successful since Casey's pancreas was inflamed. Casey's Vet was away for the day. The staff at the clinic promised to look after Casey and call the following morning with the advice of the doctor. We were all worried. Gabriela came upstairs to our place and visited. Together we watched television in an attempt to take our minds off Casey. Even though we prayed for the return of *Good Health* for Casey, there was a part of me that knew my prayer was biased and should have been for the *Well Being* of Casey. That night I was restless and did not sleep well. The next morning Gabriela called saying that the Veterinarian told her that he could operate on Casey. This was great news and seemed very promising. My faith was restored.

I went out shopping. When I returned there was no news.

They wanted to know if they should wake up Casey so I could say good bye. I told them "No, waking up Casey would be cruel. She is already at peace. Let Casey remain at peace. Put Casey down so she won't suffer."

Two hours later there was a knock at the back door. I opened the door and Gabriela stood before me. With tears running down her cheeks she sobbed, "They opened Casey up and discovered that she had cancer of the pancreas, and there was little hope for her. Even if they did another operation to remove the cancer the operation might not succeed, and Casey would probably only have a very short while to live. With this news, I asked the doctor to put Casey down. They wanted to know if they should wake up Casey so I could say good bye. I told them "No, waking up Casey would be cruel. She is already at peace. Let Casey remain at peace. Put Casey down so she won't suffer."

We all cried and consoled each other for the loss of the *Sweetest Dog in the Whole Wide World!*

Together we read the poem about Rainbow Bridge. Reading the poem helped soothe our aching hearts. Gabriela knew Casey was happy at Rainbow Bridge, and would be waiting for her when her time came. Meanwhile, we all realized that whatever had gotten lodged in Casey's tummy was a blessing in disguise. Because of the obstruction, she did not have to suffer months of slow pain and the torture that accompanies dying of cancer. Right up to her end, Casey was surrounded by love. Casey deserved the best!

Fortunately, we survivors had each other for comfort.

Beyond co-incidence, a local full service funeral provider was having a memorial service that evening for anyone who had lost someone dear to them over the past couple of years. My friend, Jan, who is Mother of Lacee, was going with me to the memorial service. Realizing she would have two people to go with her, Gabriela said she would accompany us. I called the Funeral Director named Julie Evans, and since it was a candlelight service Julie added a special candle for Casey. Before the service, Julie befriended Gabriela offering her special condolences. The memorial service was the perfect last touch for a perfectly wonderful dog who had graced our lives…*the Sweetest Dog in the Whole Wide World.*

Casey will live on in our hearts forever. I plan on asking Gabriela if it will be alright if I put Casey's picture up next to the picture of Max. Max is the dog that Raymond and I owned that we lost about fourteen months ago (you can read his story—it is called *Who is in Charge)*. Max's picture graces our entrance hallway so that his spirit oversees and blesses all the dogs who are visiting their "home away from home." I believe that Casey has earned a place alongside Max. Together they will live on blessing all the dogs who enter this house. In return, of course, Max and Casey will be blessed.

For those of you who may not know the Rainbow Bridge prayer, I include it because it is inspiring, heart-warming, and has certainly helped me.

Just this side of heaven is a place
called Rainbow Bridge.

When an animal dies that has been
especially close to someone here,
that pet goes to Rainbow Bridge.
There are meadows and hills for all
of our special friends so they can run
and play together. There is plenty of
food, water and sunshine, and our
friends are warm and comfortable

All the animals who had been ill and
old are restored to health and vigor.
Those who were hurt or maimed are
made whole and strong again, just as
we remember them in our dreams of
days and times gone by. The animals
are happy and content, except for
one small thing; they each miss
someone very special to them, who
had to be left behind.

They all run and play together, but
the day comes when one suddenly
stops and looks into the distance. His
bright eyes are intent. His eager
body quivers. Suddenly he begins to
run from the group, flying over the
green grass, his legs carrying him
faster and faster.

You have been spotted, and when
you and your special friend finally
meet, you cling together in joyous
reunion, never to be parted again.
The happy kisses rain upon your

141

face; your hands again caress the beloved head, and you look once more into the trusting eyes of your pet, so long gone from your life but never absent from your heart.

Then you cross Rainbow Bridge together....

Author unknown

Who Is the Author,
Blenda R. Pilon

Blenda was born in Jamestown, NY, and grew up in Westchester County, a prestigious suburb of NYC. Blenda graduated from Indiana University in 1968 with an MSc in psychology, and later received a degree as a hypnotherapist from the American Society of Clinical Hypnosis.

The majority of Blenda's career has been in the areas of counseling and ministerial work. Blenda started off her career as a guidance counselor in a high school in Berwick, Pennsylvania, and officially ended her career some forty years later as a guidance counselor in a middle school in North Carolina. In between these years, Blenda moved to Canada where she became a dual citizen and started a private practice in Vancouver, BC, Canada called Professional Clinical Therapy specializing in relationships. In her private practice, spanning seventeen years, Blenda saw over 6,500 clients successfully. Together with her husband, Raymond, they brought into Canada the work of the renowned bestselling relationship author, Dr. John Gray and co-facilitated his relationship workshops. Blenda wrote a relationship book called *FALLING IN LOVE AND STAYING IN LOVE* that was endorsed by Dr. John Gray.

Having a strong interest in metaphysics, Blenda went on to become a minister in the Centers for Spiritual Living. With her husband, Rev Raymond Pilon, she co-facilitated as a minister in the **God Is One Center** in Virginia Beach, Virginia. A few years after retiring from the ministry, Blenda and her husband traveled. As part of their travels they went to Costa Rica and stayed there for eighteen months, living fifty meters from the Caribbean Sea where Raymond began writing his book based on forty one dreams called *The Quantum Love Gene*. During the writing of his book, Blenda helped Raymond with editing, inspiration and some marketing.

One day while in Costa Rica and walking her dog, Max, on the shores of the Caribbean Sea, a lady who was also walking her dog noticed how much fun Blenda was having with her dog. Because the lady was moving, she asked Blenda if she and her husband would house sit her home and dog sit her dog. Blenda and Raymond accepted. This started their dog sitting. Blenda, Raymond and their dog named Max enjoyed meeting new dogs for whom they would give care. They loved them and treated the dogs in their charge as family members.

Four years later when back in Canada, Max passed away. Blenda decided that she wanted to stop house sitting and strictly do dog sitting. She said, "I have placed the picture of Max in the front entrance hallway of our new home. He will be our Spiritual Guide for all the fur balls we dog sit. Dog sitting is a way I can contribute in my semi-retirement. It is fun, and I can't think of anything I would rather be doing."

As Blenda finishes her book called ***DOG SECRETS as Whispered to the Dog Sitter***, she is already planning her next ***DOG SECRETS*** book. Blenda is going to include stories from other dog lovers about the secrets their dogs have revealed (whispered) to them. Blenda invites you to submit your stories by going to her website: **www.DogSecretsWhispered.com**. You may also email Blenda at DogSecrets1@gmail.com.

Blenda says, "I really love having dogs as part of my life. I am thrilled that my husband also enjoys dog sitting. Already these wonderful canine fur balls have taught me so much about my greatest passion. It is learning more about Unconditional Love. I am thankful, and embrace the new adventures awaiting my husband and me."

VISIT BLENDA'S WEBSITE

Check out the contests!

Submit your story!

www.DogSecretsWhispered.com

Made in the USA
Charleston, SC
07 January 2014